Into Grammar

Book 4

Donna Cocking
and
Clorinda Di Dio

Illustrated by Terry Allen

ABOUT THIS SERIES
Into Grammar is a formal English series comprising four books which accommodate all year levels in the primary school. This invaluable resource enables teachers and students to explore the essential skills of grammar, punctuation and correct language use through a comprehensive range of language-related activities.

The information provided in this series is grouped thematically. The initial language activity introduces the key concepts and the subsequent activities encourage students to extend, practise and consolidate their knowledge and skills.

TEACHERS NOTES
These extensive teachers notes include teaching focus points, supportive background information, subject integration with additional activities, and detailed answers to the activities provided.

LANGUAGE ACTIVITIES
A comprehensive range of language-related activities includes explanations, instructions, diagrams, tables, mapping, time lines, letters, advertisements, recipes, poetry, notes, games and reports. These activities focus on a part of grammar, punctuation or correct language use. They introduce a concept within a context so that students are indirectly learning about a part of speech and its function within a whole language context before attempting any isolated written activities.

GRAMMATICAL FOCUS
The activities provided incorporate the following:

Grammar:

Clauses:	principal, subordinate
Phrases:	adjectival, adverbial, noun, prepositional, verbal, participial
Sentences:	complex, compound, paragraph, predicate, simple, subject
Speech parts:	adjectives, adverbs, articles, determiners, conjunctions, nouns, prepositions, pronouns, verbs

Punctuation: apostrophes, capital letters, colons, commas, dashes, ellipses, exclamation marks, hyphens, question marks, quotation marks, semicolons

Correct Usage: abbreviations, antonyms, collocations, colloquial terms, contractions, compound words, homonyms, homophones, idioms, plurals, redundancies, repetitions, root words, similes, singular, synonyms

Copyright © Donna Cocking and Clorinda Di Dio
Illustrated by Terry Allen

First published in 1995 by LEARNING SOLUTIONS
ISBN 1 86399 087 9

Acknowledgements
With all Learning Solutions publications every attempt is made to acknowledge copyright. Any infringements are purely coincidental and the publisher offers apologies where applicable.

Into Grammar

Book 4

Pages	Contents

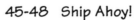

READY REFERENCE (including teachers notes pages)

PAGES	TITLE	LANGUAGE ACTIVITIES	GRAMMATICAL FOCUS
5-8	FIND IT IN THE CLASSIFIEDS GET ADVERTISED! CLASSY CAMERAS AND CARS	INDEX FORMAT ADVERTISEMENT WRITING SENTENCE COMPLETION	ABBREVIATIONS ABBREVIATIONS PRINCIPAL AND SUBORDINATE CLAUSES
9-12	BOO TO ZOOS SPOT THE PREPOSITION FILL UP ON PHRASES	ARGUMENT FORMAT CLOZE REPORT	TEXT STRUCTURE PREPOSITIONS ADJECTIVAL AND ADVERBIAL PHRASES
13-16	HOUSE AND HOME THE GREENHOUSE EFFECT HOUSEWORK	PICTURE CLUES TABLE COMPLETION DESCRIPTIVE SENTENCES	COMPOUND WORDS TENSE, IRREGULAR AND REGULAR VERBS VERBS
17-20	PREFERRED POSITIONS PLANTING PHRASES BLANKETY BLANKS	INTERPRETING TABLES DIAGRAM COMPLETION SURVEY	PARTICIPIAL PHRASES PREPOSITIONAL PHRASES COLLOCATION
21-24	ON DISPLAY BARE YOUR TEETH WHERE DO THEY COME FROM?	MUSEUM TAGS NOTE TAKING MAPPING	ADVERBS AND ADJECTIVES TEXT STRUCTURE COMMON NOUNS, PROPER NOUNS
25-28	TIMELY TRIVIA TO PASS THE TIME OF DAY THE PRESENT FROM THE PAST	TIME LINE TIME FRAMES VERB SLEUTH	PAST PARTICIPLES PRESENT PARTICIPLES, DETERMINERS INFINITIVES, TENSE
29-32	DINNERTIME FOR PLANTS GETTING DOWN TO THE GRASS ROOTS BEFORES AND AFTERS	EXPLANATION WORD SLEUTH CLASSIFICATION	PARAGRAPHS ROOT WORDS PREFIXES AND SUFFIXES
33-36	SUPER SPINACH SAPS SAILOR'S STRENGTH! THIS IS A PIECE OF CAKE A SMORGASBORD OF FOOD	FORMAL LETTER LITERAL MEANING CROSSWORD	PUNCTUATION IDIOMS WORD ORIGINS
37-40	THE STORY OF A BASEBALL PLAYER WHICH PART OF SPEECH? OPPOSITES ATTRACT	BIOGRAPHY TABLE COMPLETION TAG WORD SEARCH	SEQUENCING PARTS OF SPEECH SYNONYMS AND ANTONYMS
41-44	ANNUAL GENERAL MEETING HOW WAS IT SAID? MIXED-UP RIDDLES	MEETING MINUTES SPEECH BUBBLES PROVERBS	TEXT STRUCTURE, FORMAT MOOD TEXT ORGANISATION
45-48	SHIP AHOY! TREASURE ON TRIGGER ISLAND	DIARY ENTRY GAME	SUBJECT AND VERB AGREEMENT SUBJECT AND PREDICATE
49-52	GET AWAY TO CORAL ISLAND! P.S. I MISS YOU! INDIRECTLY SPEAKING	TRAVEL ADVERTISEMENT POSTCARD CONVERSATIONS	COLONS AND SEMICOLONS SIMILES QUOTATION MARKS, INDIRECT SPEECH
53-56	READ THE LABEL SPAGHETTI SAUCE VERB EXPRESS	INFORMATION LABELS INSTRUCTIONS MATCHING MEANINGS	MAIN IDEA TRANSITIVE AND INTRANSITIVE VERBS ACTIVE AND PASSIVE VOICE
57-60	BY PHONE OR FAX GREETINGS THERE'S A BETTER WAY TO SAY IT	SHORTHAND LANGUAGE NOTES AND MESSAGES APPROPRIATE LANGUAGE USE	TERMS AND ABBREVIATIONS CORRECT USAGE SYNONYMS, DICTIONARY SKILLS

Teachers Notes

Find it in the Classifieds

Focus Points
- To use the index of a classified advertisement section of a newspaper.
- To write advertisements for a newspaper.
- To identify abbreviations commonly used in the classified advertisements.
- To identify principal and subordinate clauses in sentences.
- To finish an advertisement by adding clauses.

Background Information
Classified Advertisements
Classified advertisements are always brief. Abbreviations are usually used and whole sentences are not necessary. Only important, relevant information is given.

Clauses
A clause is a group of words within a sentence which contains a finite verb and its subject. The principal clause is the most important part of the sentence. It makes sense by itself. Every sentence contains at least one principal clause.

> _I found the pencil_ which had been broken.

A subordinate clause adds meaning to the principal clause and can not stand on its own.
> I ate the cake _which mum made._

Subject Integration
Maths: Students study the classified advertisements in a newspaper. They then tally the number of advertisements in each category. Students find the cost of advertising per line and calculate the price of some advertisements.

Art and Craft: Students look at different ads in newspapers and magazines. They then choose a product and design an advertisement for it.

Language: Make a class classified advertisements book. Each child writes an advertisement for the book.

Answers
Find it in the Classifieds
Metro, Hosp, Appoints, 4WDs
(a) 93 (b) 78 or 79 (c) 91 (d) 92 (e) 82 (f) 98 (g) 105
1. 90 2. 104 3. 80 4. 97

Get Advertised
1. Immaculate brick and tile home in superb location. 4 bedrooms, 2 bathrooms. double garage.

2. 2 bedroom, two storey town house. Modern decor, enclosed patio, double carport.

Classy Cameras and Cars
because it can go anywhere, so it is easy to carry, as the great outdoors, when you're going to the beach, and never miss a great outdoors shot again
1. _I saw the movie_ (which was very scary).
2. _My brother bought a computer_ (that is very sophisticated).
3. _The car_ (which I wanted to buy) _is in very good condition._
4. _They will buy a house_ (if they win the lottery).
5. _Did you buy the car_ (that was advertised in the paper)?

Learning Solutions

Find it in the Classifieds

Look at this index for the Classified Advertisement section of a newspaper. Underline the abbreviated form for some words. Answer the questions below.

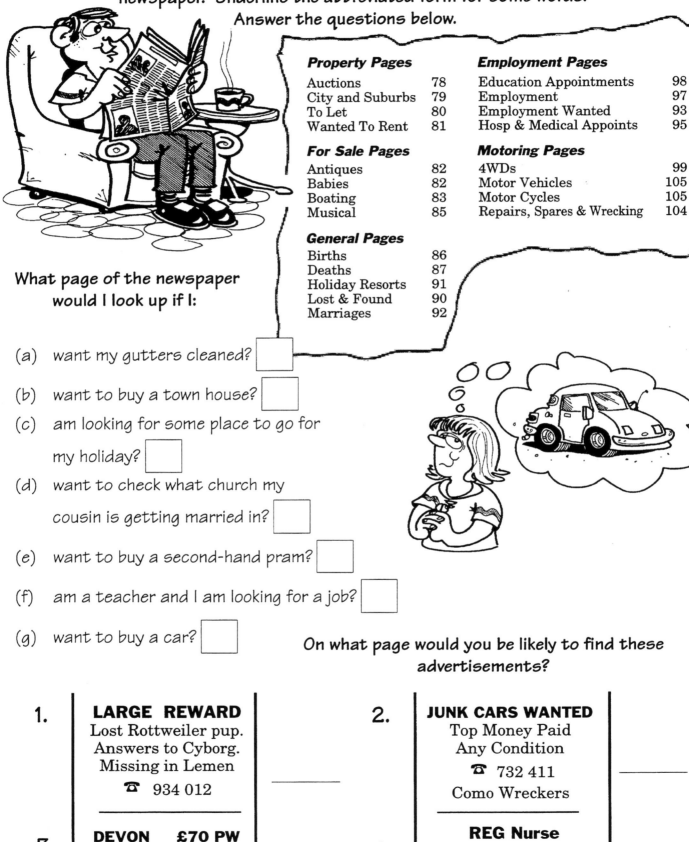

Property Pages

Auctions	78
City and Suburbs	79
To Let	80
Wanted To Rent	81

For Sale Pages

Antiques	82
Babies	82
Boating	83
Musical	85

General Pages

Births	86
Deaths	87
Holiday Resorts	91
Lost & Found	90
Marriages	92

Employment Pages

Education Appointments	98
Employment	97
Employment Wanted	93
Hosp & Medical Appoints	95

Motoring Pages

4WDs	99
Motor Vehicles	105
Motor Cycles	105
Repairs, Spares & Wrecking	104

What page of the newspaper would I look up if I:

(a) want my gutters cleaned? ☐

(b) want to buy a town house? ☐

(c) am looking for some place to go for my holiday? ☐

(d) want to check what church my cousin is getting married in? ☐

(e) want to buy a second-hand pram? ☐

(f) am a teacher and I am looking for a job? ☐

(g) want to buy a car? ☐

On what page would you be likely to find these advertisements?

1.

LARGE REWARD
Lost Rottweiler pup.
Answers to Cyborg.
Missing in Lemen
☎ 934 012

_____

2.

JUNK CARS WANTED
Top Money Paid
Any Condition
☎ 732 411
Como Wreckers

_____

3.

DEVON   £70 PW
House, 3 beds,
close to shops
☎ 345 298

_____

4.

REG Nurse
Needed for night duty
3-4 nights per week
☎ 734 986

_____

Learning Solutions

Get Advertised !

Write advertisements for the following situations under the correct category.

1. Your mum just had a baby boy.
2. You're selling the family car.
3. You found a gold watch in the park.
4. You are a carpenter looking for work.

BIRTHS	LOST AND FOUND
EMPLOYMENT WANTED	MOTOR VEHICLES

Immac b/t home
in superb loc
4 beds, 2 baths,
dble gge

---

2 storey t/house
2 beds, Mod dec, encl
patio, dble c/port

Study these advertisements which have been written in abbreviated form. Rewrite the advertisements in full.

_____

_____

_____

_____

_____

_____

_____

_____

Write an advertisement to sell your house.
Use as many abbreviations as possible.

Classified ad.

_____
_____
_____

Learning Solutions

CLASSY
CAMERAS AND CARS

Find the subordinate clauses in the advertisement below and underline them.

The fantastic **BONUS P1** is a special camera because it can go anywhere. It is as rugged as the great outdoors. This camera is light so it is easy to carry. Take the **P1** with you when you're going to the beach. It's water resistant to a depth of 5 metres.

Buy the **BONUS P1** and never miss a great outdoors shot again.

Underline the principal clauses and circle the subordinate clauses in the sentences below.

1. I saw the movie which was very scary.
2. My brother bought a computer that is very sophisticated.
3. The car which I wanted to buy was in very good condition.
4. They will buy a house if they win the lottery.
5. Did you buy the car that was advertised in the paper?

Complete the advertisement. Finish the sentences written by adding subordinate clauses and then write two more sentences of your own.

The **COMET Sonata** is the car for today's discerning family.

It is affordable so _____

_____

It has an impressive list of standard features which _____

_____

_____

_____

_____

Contact your local **COMET** dealer who _____

_____

Teachers Notes

Boo to Zoos

Focus Points
- To identify the main points of an argument.
- To write an argument given a structure to follow.
- To identify prepositions in sentences and to apply the correct preposition to certain words.
- To write phrases which add meaning to sentences.
- To identify adjectival and adverbial phrases.

Background Information
Argument
In an argument the writer presents their point of view on a topic. An argument can follow this framework:
- Introduction - the issue is stated and the point of view given.
- Evidence - reasons are given why the writer feels this way.
- Conclusion - a re-statement of the writer's position on the topic.

Prepositions
Prepositions are words that show the relationship between nouns and pronouns in a sentence. Prepositions often begin phrases. There are many prepositions. Some examples are:

with, up, into, during, in, from, after, through, across, for, inside, beside.

Some words must be followed by certain prepositions only:

disapprove of, different from, accompanied by, similar to, sympathise with.

Phrases
A phrase is a group of words that does not contain a finite verb.
A phrase can start with either a preposition, a participle or an infinitive.
The bench was <u>beside the tree.</u> (prepositional phrase)
The people <u>standing in line</u> were getting angry. (participial phrase)
The giraffe lay down <u>to have a sleep</u>. (infinitive)
Phrases that add meaning to nouns are called adjectival phrases. *The monkey <u>with the sore foot</u> screeched loudly.*
Phrases that add meaning to verbs are called adverbial phrases. <u>*With great speed*</u>, *the bird flew away.*
Both adverbial and adjectival phrases begin with prepositions. Phrases should be written as close as possible to the words they are describing.

Subject Integration
Language: Students work with a partner and write opposing arguments for a topic such as 'Homework should be banned'. Students look at a partner's work and add meaning to their sentences by using phrases where appropriate. Students write a letter to the editor of a newspaper giving their views on the slaughtering of elephants in Africa.
Social Studies: Brainstorm animals which fall under the extinct, endangered, rare and vulnerable categories. Each student researches and writes a report on an endangered animal. Students find out what conservation and breeding programmes and policies have been implemented at their local zoo.
Art/Craft: Students design an advertisement for their local zoo. Students design a poster about wildlife conservation.

Answers
Boo to Zoos
1. Animals should be left in their own environment
2. Some zoos provide inadequate enclosures.
3. Some animals are difficult to breed in captivity.
Spot the Preposition: 1. in 2. by, of 3. of, for 4. of 5. in 6. for, on
Spot the Preposition Cont.: 1. among 2. with 3. of 4. to 5. for 6. by 7. from 8. in
Fill Up On Phrases
1. for the animals 2. from 10 a.m. 3. in the zoo 4. with the long arms 5. from Africa
6. by the sea
     Adjectival: in the zoo, with the long arms, from Africa
     Adverbial: for the animals, from 10 a.m. by the sea

Learning Solutions

Boo to Zoos

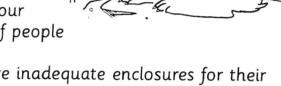

Read the argument below.

I believe that no animal should be kept in a zoo. Firstly, how can animals be happy living in captivity when they could be roaming free in their own natural environment? How would you like to spend your days being ogled and stared at by hundreds of people without being able to escape or hide?

Secondly, a large number of zoos still have inadequate enclosures for their animals. These animals suffer as a result of their cramped living conditions which indirectly affect their health.

Finally, some animals are extremely difficult to breed in captivity. So when they die they will be replaced by another of that species which will need to be taken from the wild.

I strongly believe that it is immoral for us to impose our will on these animals for our own personal gratification and entertainment.

Write the three main points that support the argument above.

1._____

2._____

3._____

Now write three points that would support the opposite view, that is, that zoos are great places. You can choose some ideas from the box below or write some of your own.

zoos carry out valuable research, they educate the public, initiate breeding programs for endangered species, provide relaxation and entertainment for the public

1._____

2._____

3._____

On the back of this sheet, use the points you have written above to write an argument. Write an introduction and a conclusion as well as presenting some of your previous points.

Learning Solutions

S⦿⦁⦁T the Preposition

Underline the prepositions in these sentences from the argument.

1. I believe that no animal should be kept in a zoo.
2. How would you like to be ogled by hundreds of people.
3. A large number of zoos have inadequate enclosures for their animals.
4. These animals suffer as a result of their cramped living conditions.
5. Some animals are extremely difficult to breed in captivity.
6. It is immoral for us to impose our will on these animals.

Fill in the spaces below with the correct prepositions. Use the words in the box below.

> by, in, with, for, of, among, from, to

1. The zoo keeper gave the three monkeys some food to share _____ themselves.
2. The attendant was very angry_____ the visitor.
3. I disapprove _____ keeping animals in captivity.
4. The snake is similar _____ the one I saw in my back yard.
5. The animal activist was grateful _____ the award he received.
6. The elephants were accompanied _____ their keeper on their walk around the zoo.
7. The female gibbon had to be isolated _____the other gibbons in the enclosure.
8. The South Croft Zoo takes great pride _____ its successful breeding program.

Complete these sentences using prepositional phrases.

1. The monkey scampered across _____ .
2. The lion was sleeping peacefully with _____ .
3. The otter in _____ was swimming and diving.
4. Around _____ birds were nesting.
5. The baby possum slept during _____

FILL UP ON PHRASES

Read the passage below about the African elephant. Write phrases in the spaces to add meaning to the sentences.

The African elephant is the largest land dwelling animal _____ .
In the wild it is found _____ . Sadly, people killed elephants_____ and captured them
_____ .

In the 1980s an average of 80 000 elephants were killed _____ .
Fortunately, many people who loved elephants worked hard to try _____ . Today laws protect elephants _____
_____ . Many countries
_____ have now prohibited ivory imports and this has reduced the slaughter.

Underline the phrases in these sentences.

1. Zoo keepers care for the animals.
2. The zoo is open from 10 a.m.
3. The giraffes in the zoo are young.
4. The orang-utan with the long arms climbed skillfully.
5. The zebra from Africa died.
6. Penguins live by the sea.

Write the phrases from the exercise above under their correct category below.

ADJECTIVAL PHRASES	ADVERBIAL PHRASES
_____	_____
_____	_____
_____	_____

Learning Solutions

Teachers Notes

House and Home

Focus Points
- To solve picture clues using infinitive phrases.
- To identify irregular and regular verbs.

Background Information
Regular Verbs
Only the ending of a regular verb is altered to form another tense: 's', 'es', 'ed', 'd', 't' or 'ing'. For example: *to kiss – kisses, kissing, kissed, kiss.* Most verbs are regular.

Irregular Verbs
Some irregular verbs change form dramatically when forming another tense.
For example: *to be – am, is, are, being, was, were, been, be.*

Tense
Verbs change form according to the tense expressed. The tense indicates the period of time in which an action takes place and for how long that action occurs.

Simple tenses:
Present Tense: *I **am** at the zoo.*
Past Tense: *Yesterday I **was** at the zoo.*
Future Tense: *Tomorrow I **will be** at the zoo.*

Complex forms:
- Continuous – includes the verb 'to be' and the present participle, indicating a continuing action or event.
Present Continuous: *She **is going** to the zoo.*
Past Continuous: *She **was going** to the zoo.*
Future Continuous: *She **will be going** to the zoo.*
- Perfect – includes the verb 'to have' and the past participle, indicating that the action or event is complete.
Present Perfect: *She **has been** at the zoo.*
Past Perfect: *She **had been** at the zoo.*
Future Perfect: *She **will have been** at the zoo.*
- Perfect Continuous – combination of the perfect and continuous forms, including the verbs 'to be' and 'to have' with a participle.
Present Perfect Continuous: *She **has been going** to the zoo.*
Past Perfect Continuous: *She **had been going** to the zoo.*
Future Perfect Continuous: *She **will have been going** to the zoo.*

Subject Integration
Language
Which Tense?
Have students discuss the context clues which indicate the tense of the verb in the sentences given in THE GREENHOUSE EFFECT. For example, in **Yesterday**, Mrs Davis **wore** or **was wearing** her green housecoat outside, the verb **to wear** must be in the past tense because the action agrees with what happened **Yesterday**.
Brainstorm lists of regular and irregular verbs.

Answers
HOUSE AND HOME
to be homesick, to bring the house down, to home in on, to be housebroken, to be homeward bound, to do homework
homework, houseboat, housemaid, homestead, houselights, homespun

THE GREENHOUSE EFFECT
Irregular verbs: to run (run, ran, will run), to eat (eat, will eat), to have (have, had, will have), to ring (ring, rang, will ring), to fly (fly, flew, will fly), to drive (drive, drove, will drive), to write (write, wrote, will write)
Regular verbs: to live (live, lived, will live), to jump (jump, jumped, will jump), to lock (lock, locked, will lock)
Complex forms are acceptable answers, however, simple forms of tense for each verb are:
1) promised 2) will give 3) gave 4) wore 5) hired 6) warned 7) bought 8) likes 9) grew 10) lives 11) brought 12) will go

HOUSEWORK
Verbs: scrape, climb, swing, carry, drive, cover, mix, lay, wear, cut, build, dig

House and Home

Use some of these phrases to solve the picture clues.

to home in on, to be homesick, to do homework, to be homeward bound, to be like a home away from home, to bring the house down.

= an ear, which means to 'sound like'

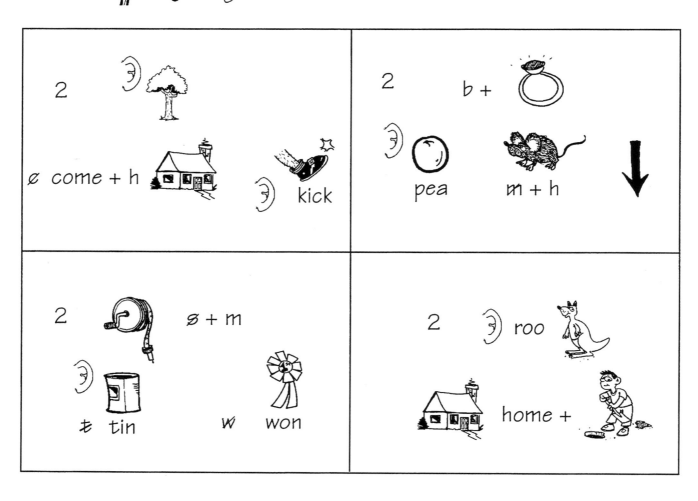

Add home or house to these words. Complete the explanations for each.

_home_____ land — your place or country of origin.

_____ work — the completion of _____

_____ boat — _____

_____ maid — _____

_____ stead — the principal _____

_____ lights — the lights _____

_____ spun

Use some of these home or house words to create your own picture clues.

The Greenhouse Effect

Complete the table below. Tick the box to indicate irregular verbs.

Infinitive	Present Tense	Past Tense	Future Tense
☐ to run	I run	I ran	I will run
☐ to eat		I ate	
☐ to have			I will have
☐ to live	I live		
☐ to ring		I rang	
☐ to jump			
☐ to fly			
☐ to drive	I drive		
☐ to lock			I will lock
☐ to write		I wrote	

Read each sentence carefully, then write the correct form for each verb.

1) The pet shop owner (to promise) _____ the puppy was house-trained.
2) The neighbours (to give) _____ Mr Johnson a house-warming when he moves into the neighbourhood.
3) Last night the owner (to give) _____ us a hamburger on the house.
4) Yesterday Mrs Davis (to wear) _____ her green housecoat outside.
5) Mum (to hire) _____ a new housekeeper last week.
6) Many years ago, a scientist (to warn) _____ the loggers about the greenhouse effect.
7) We went to the estate agent and (to buy) _____ a home unit.
8) Kate's father (to like) _____ to fly homing pigeons every Saturday.
9) Milly said that she (to grow) _____ her prize-winning orchids in a greenhouse.
10) The president of the USA (to live) _____ in the White House.
11) The audience clapped so loudly that they nearly (to bring) _____ the house down.
12) Tomorrow we (to go) _____ to the Houses of Parliament.

Housework

Look at this picture of a building site.

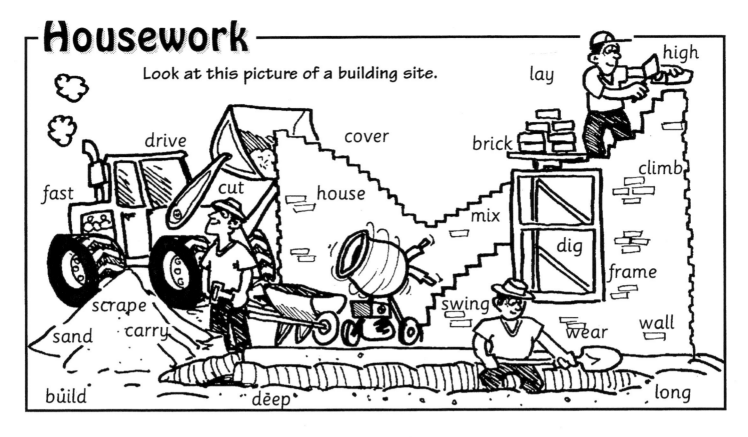

Write the verbs on the bricks below.

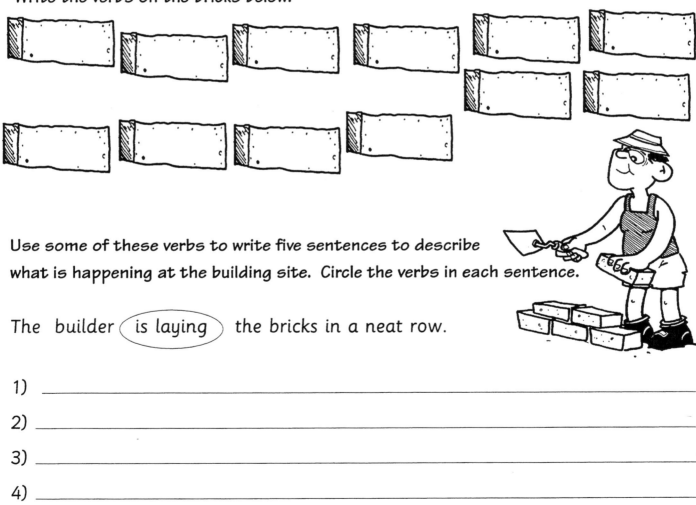

Use some of these verbs to write five sentences to describe what is happening at the building site. Circle the verbs in each sentence.

The builder (is laying) the bricks in a neat row.

1) _____

2) _____

3) _____

4) _____

5) _____

Teachers Notes

Preferred Positions

Focus Points
- To use the information in a table to write descriptive phrases.
- To label a map with sentences which include prepositional phrases.
- To survey friends and analyse responses to a word association activity.

Background Information
Phrases
A phrase is always part of a sentence or a clause. A phrase is an arrangement of words without a finite verb. Infinite verbs have no subject – *to run home, to hop away,* whereas finite verbs have a subject – *the boy jumped, a rabbit hops.*
Phrases can perform the tasks of many parts of speech. Phrases can be prepositional, adverbial, participial, adjectival, verbal or noun. That is, they elaborate on the work done by nouns, pronouns, adverbs, verbs, adjectives and prepositions. Phrases do not stand alone as they rely on other parts of a sentence or a clause for meaning.

Prepositional and Participial Phrases
The most common phrases begin with a preposition or a participle.
Prepositional phrases: *in the sea, on the shelf, under the bridge*
Participial Phrases with:
1) Present Participle – *running very quickly, feeling sad, coming slowly*
2) Past Participle – *packed with meat, booked for speeding, seated on the bench*

Collocation
Collocation means to put things together in a meaningful order, to match. Certain words and phrases go together, such as *salt and pepper, as white as snow, blue moon.* Similar to word association, collocation refers to the joining of these words.

Subject Integration
Writing
Newspaper Search: Underline individual phrases found in newspaper or magazine articles and indicate whether they are adjectival, adverbial or noun phrases.
Phrase Garden: Students write phrases on large cardboard flower templates. Attach bamboo skewers to the back of flowers. Plant in old pots filled with soil. Have students choose flowers from the garden and use several phrases as ideas for story writing.
Wanted Poster: Students write individual descriptive phrases on pieces of paper, such as – *with black hair, with an eye patch, in a terrible voice, running from the crime scene.* Crumple and place paper pieces in a lucky dip box. Students draw papers and create a wanted poster from the descriptions given on their papers. They highlight or bold the phrases used on their poster.
Blankety Blanks Survey:
Analyse the results of the survey. Did any participants answer incorrectly? If so, why? Discuss the relevance of the context clues. Examine the extent to which context clues, background knowledge and cultural experiences contribute to a person's understanding. For instance, would you have difficulty reading a computer manual if you'd never seen a computer? Or, would you know the answer to bacon and *"blank"* if you'd lived your life in a jungle?

Answers
Blankety Blanks
bacon and eggs, salt and pepper, bread and butter, curry and rice, knife and fork, chair and table, dustpan and brush, up and down, in and out, left and right, stop and go, entry and exit
Survey: apple pie and ice-cream, coffee and after dinner mints, spaghetti and meat-balls, steak and kidney pie

Preferred Positions

Use this information to write phrases to describe these plants.

Planting Table

full sun ⚪	well-drained soil ▢	wind resistant •◦
part sun ◍	moist soil ▨	frost resistant ✳
full shade ●	very wet soil ■	sun resistant ✡

Plant Description

Plants for containers

Flowers for cutting

Plants with fragrant flowers

Groundcover plants for sun

Plants for water

Plant Types

Bulbs – Daffodils (yellow and white) ◍ ▢ •◦

Perennials – Chrysanthemums (multi-coloured) ⚪ ✡ ▨ •◦

Shrubs – Roses (various colours) ◍ ▨ •◦ ✡

Climbers – Sweet Pea (pink/purple and red) ⚪ ▢ ✡

Water Plants – Yellow Water Lily (yellow) ■ ●

Daffodils: *with white and yellow flowers, ideal for containers, preferring part shade, moist soil, not frost resistant*

Chrysanthemums: _____

_____

Roses: _____

_____

Sweet Pea: _____

_____

Use these participial phrases to create descriptive sentences.

- **by the intense sunlight   +   Crumpling ...**
Crumpling beneath our feet were the dead leaves that had been burnt by the intense sunlight.

- **a golden coin wedged in the sand + Walking carefully ...**

_____

- **in the luxurious rich soil   +   Covered ...**

_____

- **drank the cool spring water   +   Feeling ...**

_____

Learning Solutions

Planting Phrases

Use some of these phrases to complete this design for an outdoor garden area.

in the ground
in pots or containers
between the paving
over the pergola
near the pathway
near the tap

under the verandah
in the pond
among the weeds
around the tree
across from the herbs
beneath the window

You are planting:
- herbs, lawn, ferns, waterlilies, petunias, pansies (annuals)
- daffodils, irises (bulbs)
- hibiscus, camellias (shrubs)
- jasmine, wisteria (climbers)

Write a sentence to describe where each will be planted and underline the phrases.

verandah

pergola

greenhouse

The ferns will go in the greenhouse.

window

paving

pot

container

pond

garden bed	pathway

garden bed

BLANKETY BLANKS

Complete these well-known pairs. Write your own examples for each category.

INSTRUCTIONS

up and _____

in and _____

left and _right_____

stop and _____

entry and _____

_____

_____

FOOD PAIRS

bacon and _____

salt and _____

bread and _____

curry and _____

_____

_____

HOUSEHOLD ITEMS

knife and _____

chair and _____

dustpan and _____

_____

_____

**Survey five friends for answers to these pairs.
Record the responses below.**

A1 apple pie and _____ cream   **A2** coffee and after _____ mints

A3 spaghetti and _____ balls   **A4** steak and _____ pie

NAMES	ANSWERS: A1	A2	A3	A4
1.				
2				
3.				
4.				
5.				

Survey another five friends for answers to these pairs. Record the responses below.

B1 apple pie and _____   **B2** coffee and _____

B3 spaghetti and _____   **B4** steak and _____

NAMES	ANSWERS: B1	B2	B3	B4
1.				
2.				
3.				
4.				
5.				

On Display

Focus Points
- To identify the adverbs and adjectives in sentences.
- To label a world map with names of animals to show places of origin.

Background Information
Adverbs
An adverb chiefly enhances the meaning of a verb. Adverbs describe how, where and when an action occurred. Adverbs can modify an adjective or another adverb but not a noun.
Many adverbs end in 'ly' — *quickly, slowly, loudly*.
Adjectives
An adjective chiefly enhances the meaning of a noun or pronoun. Adjectives describe the appearance of a person, place or thing. Types of adjectives include:
> Possessive: my, your, our, his, her, its, their
> Distributive: each, every, some, neither, either
> Demonstrative: this, these, those, that
> Numbers or Order: five, fifth, last, next, first
> Interrogative: which, what, whose

Answers
On Display
Adverbs and adjectives have not been repeated in the answers for each animal.
Adjectives
Llama — Peruvian, domestic, smaller, no humps, swaggering, soft-cushioned, leathery, two, long, slender, small, pointy, thick, woolly, soft, pure white, brown, black.
Deer — small, woodland, honey-coloured, thicker, darker, stark white, warning, succulent, green, long, open, shy, elusive, mating.
Hercules Beetle — one, largest, rain, rotting, strong, powerful, biting, upper, long, sharp.
Ocelot — leopard-like, short, tawny-yellow, dark, irregular, black, natural, rain, long, streamlined, slender, short, cup-shaped, small, farming.
Polar Bear — 2.7, great, creamy-white, bear, long, thick coat, bitter, cold, icy, slippery, slender, powerful, partly webbed, longer, small, pointy, floating.
Walrus — three, huge, fin-footed, sea, two, long, sharp, defensive, powerful, thick, craggy, wrinkly, bitter, rocky, shallow.
Adverbs
Llama — much, very
Deer — easily, erect, quickly
Hercules Beetle — usually, mainly
Ocelot — commonly, beautifully, strikingly, easily, fairly, erect, most, occasionally
Polar Bear — about, effortlessly, easily, quickly
Walrus — closely, chiefly, casually

Bare Your Teeth
powerful — limbs of the polar bear
long — the limbs, neck and ears of the llama; the upper jaw of the beetle; walrus tusks; coat, neck and limbs of polar bear; body of ocelot
slender — the tail of the ocelot, limbs of llama

Where Do They Come From?
1. The ocelot, white-tailed deer, Hercules beetle and llama will be in the North and South American display. 2. Arctic Circle. Walrus, Arctic Hare, Ermine, Fox, Grizzly Bear, Lemming, Wolf and Wolverine.
3. Acceptable answers may include:
- The cuscus is native to New Guinea.
- The kangaroo is native to Australia.
- The yak is native to the Tibetan Highlands.
- The lemur is native to Madagascar.
- The llama is native to South America.
- The polar bear is native to the Arctic Circle.
- The giant panda is native to central China.
- The jackdaw is native to Europe.
- The Kiwi bird is native to New Zealand.
- The giraffe is native to Africa.
- The Bengal tiger is native to Bengal.
- The Manx cat is native to the Isle of Man.
- The moose is native to North America.
- The orang-utan is native to Indonesia.
- The komodo dragon is native to Komodo Island.
- The macaque monkey is native to Asia.

These are the signs for the new animals on display in the University Museum. Read each sign. Underline the adjectives and circle the adverbs.

On Display

OCELOT (field tiger)
PHYLUM – Chordata
ORDER – Mammalia

The ocelot is a leopard-like cat commonly found in North and South America. Its short, tawny-yellow fur is beautifully marked with dark rings and irregular, black stripes. Although strikingly marked, the ocelot easily blends into the natural vegetation of the rain forest. The ocelot has a long, streamlined body with a fairly long, slender tail. Its short, cup-shaped ears stand erect on its head. Like the fox, the ocelot is most active at night, preying on rabbits, fieldmice and small deer. Occasionally, like the fox, the ocelot can be found hunting chickens and ducks in farming areas.

LLAMA (Lama gama)
PHYLUM – Chordata
ORDER – Mammalia

Known as the 'Peruvian sheep', the llama is the domestic animal of South America. Related to the camel, the llama is much smaller and has no humps. Many features similar to that of the camel include the swaggering walk and the soft-cushioned, leathery pads on the underside of the two toes. The llama has long, slender limbs, a very long neck, a small head, and long, pointy ears. Its thick, woolly coat is soft hair which ranges in colour from pure white to brown and through to black.

POLAR BEAR (Thalarctos Maritimus)
PHYLUM – Chordata
ORDER – Mammalia

Measuring about 2.7 metres in length, the polar bear is the great, creamy-white swimmer of the bear family. It has a long, thick coat of fur which protects it from its habitat among the bitter, cold icy floes of the Arctic Circle. The soles of its feet are covered in hair which provides protection against the cold and helps to grip on the slippery ice. It has long, slender, powerful limbs, and partly webbed feet which enable it to propel effortlessly through the water. It has a much longer neck than other bears, with a rather small, pointy head. It travels on the floating ice and dives easily into the water to search for seals and walrus cubs for food. During summer, if the ice quickly melts, the bear will travel inland to feed on vegetation.

WHITE-TAILED DEER (Odocoileus virginiannus)
PHYLUM – Chordata
ORDER – Mammalia

This small deer is a woodland animal found in North America. Its honey-coloured fur is thicker and darker in winter, but the underside of its tail remains stark white. The deer is easily startled, and when it is, the tail stands erect, exposing the white underside. As it runs from danger it quickly flicks the tail from side to side — this is a warning signal to the other deer.
The deer feeds on succulent leaves, green shoots and the long grasses of the open meadows. Although a shy, elusive deer, its antlers are used during mating season for fighting.

HERCULES BEETLE
PHYLUM – Arthropoda
ORDER – Coleoptera

One of the world's largest beetles, the Hercules Beetle is usually found in the South American rain forests. Feeding on dung, rotting bark and plant foliage, this beetle has strong, powerful, biting jaws. The upper jaw is hooked with long, sharp serrations which it mainly uses for protection.

WALRUS (Odobenus)

PHYLUM – Chordata
ORDER – Mammalia

At approximately three metres in length, this huge, fin-footed sea mammal is closely related to the seal. Its two long, sharp tusks are chiefly used for digging and scraping shellfish from the rocks. The tusks are also a defensive weapon the walrus uses against the powerful polar bears and killer whales that prey on its cubs.
A thick layer of blubber under the craggy, wrinkly skin of the walrus helps to protect it from the bitter cold. The walrus spends most of the day with the herd casually basking in the rocky outcrops of the shallow coastal waters of the Arctic Circle.

Bare Your Teeth

Complete the notes under these headings.

Camouflage and Protection
· The walrus has thick blubber to protect it from the cold.

Defence
· The Hercules beetle has a long, hooked, sharp, biting jaw.

Feeding Habits
· The walrus scrapes shellfish from the rocks.

Related Animals
· The ocelot is a leopard-like cat.

Size
· The adult polar bear is about 2.7 metres long.

Which parts of the animals are described as powerful? — the jaws of the Hercules beetle, _____

long?   the neck of the llama, _____

slender?   the tail of the ocelot, _____

List adjectives to describe this grizzly bear.

Write opposites for these adverbs.

slowly   _____
here   _____
loudly   _____
worst   _____
seldom   _____
well   _____
yes   _____
high   _____

Learning Solutions

Where Do They Come From?

Use the museum signs to answer these.

1. List the animals which will be placed on display with the others native to North and South America. _____
   _____

2. In which region of the world are the polar bear and the walrus found? _____ List other animals found in this region.
   _____

3. Complete and label the animals on the map according to their country or continent of origin.

- The cuscus is native to _____ .
- The _____ is native to Australia.
- The yak is native to _____ .
- The lemur is native to _____ .
- The _____ is native to South America.
- The polar bear is native to _____ .
- The _____ is native to central China.
- The jackdaw is native to _____ .

- The Kiwi bird is native to _____ .
- The giraffe is native to _____ .
- The Bengal tiger is native to _____ .
- The _____ is native to the Isle of Man.
- The moose is native to _____ .
- The _____ is native to Indonesia.
- The komodo dragon is native to _____ .
- The macaque monkey is native to _____ .

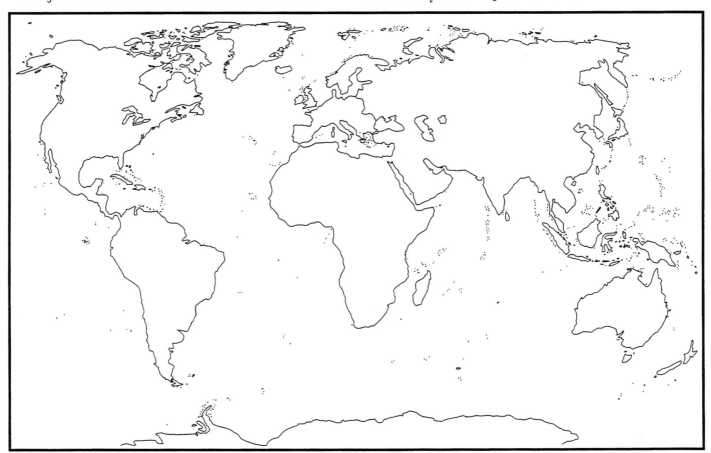

Timely Trivia

Focus Points
- To create a time line of historical events.
- To identify the past and present participles of verbs.

Background Information
Participles
Present participles are parts of verbs which describe an ongoing action – drinking, singing, dancing – in the present.

Past participles describe an action – slept, danced – in the past.

Participles can be joined with the auxiliary verbs **to have** and **to be** to make a complete verb.

The past participle of a verb is different from the past tense because it is accompanied by an auxiliary verb. In the sentence, *I drove fast*, **drove** is the past tense of the verb **to drive.** In the sentence, *She **had driven** fast*, **had driven** is the complete verb. **Had** is the auxiliary and **driven** is the past participle.

Participles can have many functions in a sentence. For example, in the phrase 'a singing *monkey*', **singing** describes the monkey (adjective), but it is also describing the actions of the monkey (verb). This present participle is therefore acting as a verbal adjective.

With the exception of irregular verbs (such as to take, to fly or to fall) the past participle is usually formed by adding 'ed' to the infinitive: *to kick – kicked.*

Determiners
Determiners are adjectives which explain nouns. The definite article **the**, indefinite articles **a** and **an** and the adjective **some** all describe nouns.

A dog can be vicious (general, indefinite as to which dog). **The** *dog is vicious* (refers to a certain dog). **Some** *dogs are vicious* (general).

Subject Integration
Verb Table

INFINITIVE to take	PAST TENSE took	PAST PARTICIPLE taken	PRESENT PARTICIPLE taking

Classification
Classify verbs as regular and irregular.

Word Web
Sort verbs into categories, RECREATION – to: fish, swim, play, run, fly, swing, jump
Plot categories onto a word web.

Answers
To Pass the Time of Day
Yesterday our neighbour was at **a** party. He had been drinking from **a** can, when **a** bee crawled out from inside **the** can and stung him on **the** lip. He went berserk. He was running around and screaming. He looked like **a** fool. He is allergic to bees. Apparently **the** last time he was stung **some** friends had to hold him down until **an/the** ambulance arrived. This time he was very lucky. We called for **an/the** ambulance and while **the** officer was examining him, his lip blew up like **a** balloon. After that he was fine. Dad said he most probably sweated all **the** poison out with **the** hysterical performance he put on for us. It must be scary though, not knowing if you're going to die from **a** tiny bee sting.

The Present From the Past
locked - to lock, running - to run, done - to do, written - to write, speaking - to speak, flown - to fly, gone - to go, lain - to lie, baking - to bake, eaten - to eat

chosen - choosing, spelt - spelling, worn - wearing, gone - going, arisen - arising

weave-wove, freeze-froze, go-went, wring-wrung, blow-blew, eat-ate, get-got, weep-wept, cling-clung, speed-sped, be-was, creep-crept, hide-hid, forgive-forgave, run-ran, draw-drew, bleed-bled, melt-melted, shoe-shod.

The customer had given the assistant her card.

Our next-door neighbour was taking his dog for a walk.

The clerk had used the computer every day.

The driver indicated as she left the kerb.

The police officer had been on leave.

The doctor was speaking to her patient.

Timely Trivia

Underline the past participle of each verb.

Cut and paste these historical events in order on a time line ranging from 1600 to 1800.

1796
Jenner discovered the smallpox vaccine.

1762
The Earl of Sandwich created the first sandwich.

1692
The Salem Witchcraft Trials started.

1617
One-way streets were introduced in London.

1695
A public drinking fountain was built in London.

1738
Cuckoo clocks were first sold in Germany.

1670
Minute hands were placed on watches in Europe.

1662
The first buses appeared in Paris.

1788
The 'First Fleet' arrived in Botany Bay.

1752
Benjamin Franklin invented a lightning conductor.

1727
Coffee was first planted in Brazil.

1756
The first chocolate factory opened in Germany.

1793
The world's first zoo opened in Paris.

1645
Wallpaper was used to decorate houses in Europe.

1606
The Union Jack became Britain's first national flag.

1702
The first daily newspaper was published in England.

1775
The American War of Independence began.

1632
The Taj Mahal had begun to be built in India.

Learning Solutions

To Pass the Time of Day

Use some of the present participles in the box below, with some of your own, to describe something that was happening to you within the time frames.

> *drinking, arising, shining, waking, throwing, taking, speaking, speeding, shaking, laying, creeping, clinging, swimming, blowing, biting, having, running, hopping, raining, driving, cutting, bringing, beginning, starting, happening, reading, saying, travelling, buying*

Date:	Time 8.00 a.m. – 10.00 a.m.

Date:	Time 11.00 a.m. – 1.00 p.m.

Date:	Time 2.00 p.m. – 4.00 p.m.

Date:	Time 5.00 p.m. – 7.00 p.m.

Use these determiners to complete.

the, a, an, some

Yesterday our neighbour was at _____ party. He had been drinking from _____ can when _____ bee crawled out from inside _____ can and stung him on _____ lip.

He went berserk. He was running around and screaming. He looked like _____ fool.

He is allergic to bees. Apparently _____ last time he was stung _____ friends had to hold him down until _____ ambulance arrived.

This time he was very lucky. We called for _____ ambulance and while _____ officer was examining him, his lip blew up like _____ balloon. After that he was fine.

Dad said he most probably sweated all _____ poison out with _____ hysterical perform-ance he put on for us.

It must be scary though, not knowing if you're going to die from _____ tiny bee sting.

The Present From the Past

Write the infinitive verb for each present and past participle.

taken	_to take_	ringing	_to ring_
locked	_____	running	_____
done	_____	written	_____
speaking	_____	flown	_____
gone	_____	lain	_____
baking	_____	eaten	_____

Circle the present participle for each past participle.

chosen	chosing	choosing	choosed	chosed
spelt	smelling	spelled	spreading	spelling
worn	wears	woring	wearing	wored
gone	going	goning	goes	goned
arisen	arised	arose	aresting	arising

Find the past tense of these verbs in the sleuth below.

z	w	k	w	r	u	n	g	w	a	s	m
f	o	r	g	a	v	e	a	t	e	c	e
r	v	w	e	n	t	b	l	e	d	r	l
o	e	h	i	d	c	l	u	n	g	e	t
z	s	h	o	d	r	e	w	q	o	p	e
e	s	p	e	d	p	w	e	p	t	t	d

weave	_____
freeze	_____
go	_____
wring	_____
blow	_____
eat	_____
get	_____
weep	_____
cling	_____
speed	_____
be	_____
creep	_____
hide	_____

forgive	_____	bleed	_____
run	_____	melt	_____
draw	_____	shoe	_____

Write the correct participle for each sentence.

The customer had (given, giving) _____ the assistant her card.

Our next-door neighbour was (taking, taken) _____ his dog for a walk.

The clerk had (using, used) _____ the computer every day.

The driver (indicating, indicated) _____ as she left the kerb.

The police officer had (been, being) _____ on leave.

The doctor was (spoken, speaking) _____ to her patient.

Learning Solutions

Teachers Notes

Dinnertime for Plants

Focus Points
- To identify the structure of an explanation.
- To write an explanation of how seeds grow.
- To locate base words in a word sleuth and match them with their correct root words.
- To match prefixes and suffixes with their base words.

Background Information
Explanation
An explanation tells us how something works or happens. It has the following features.
1. An introduction, which tells us what is being explained.
2. A description of the main features or parts. This must be written in the correct sequence.
3. An explanation of how it works.
4. A conclusion, which summarises the information and tells us about any special features.
An explanation is usually written in the present tense and contains factual information.

Prefixes, Suffixes and Root Words
Root words are words from another language which are used to form English words.
For example, *facio (I make), aqua (water), manus (hand).*
Additions can be made to the beginning or end of English words. The addition at the beginning of a word is called a **prefix** and an addition at the end is called a **suffix**. For example, *re (prefix) + write = rewrite, nation + al (suffix) = national.*

Subject Integration
Language: Students write different explanations, given a structure to follow. For example, *How to take care of plants.* Make a class book of different root words. Students add new words as they discover them.

Answers
Dinnertime for Plants
Photocopier = an instrument which uses light-sensitive photographic material to reproduce printed work.
Photography = a process which uses light to record images and produce a print or slide.
Phototherapy = using light to treat a disease.

Getting Down to the Grass Roots
Aqua = aquatic, aqualung   Portare = portable, transport
Corpus = corporal, corpse   Caput = decapitate, captain
Polis = police, politician   Pathos = sympathy, pathetic

Before and Afters
1. attract 2. transplanted 3. explain 4. disentangle 5. illegal 6. decompose
7. unusual 8. impossible 9. inside 10. reproduce
ANCE = attendance, performance   NESS = sadness, kindness, readiness   FUL = cupful, mouthful, faithful   Y = dirty, noisy, jealousy   ION = celebration, invention, confusion

Dinnertime For Plants

Read this explanation of how plants make their own food.

Plants are the only living things which can make their own food. Plants need water, air and sunlight to make food.

During the day, chlorophyll, which is the green pigment found in leaves, absorbs energy from the sun. The leaves also take in carbon dioxide from the air. The roots of the plant take in water, which then travels through the xylem vessels to the leaves. Using the energy it absorbed from the sun, the plant turns the carbon dioxide and the water into food.

The process by which plants make their food is called PHOTOSYNTHESIS.

Write a paragraph which explains how seeds grow into new plants. Use the notes below to help you.

Process is called germination. There is a food store inside the seed. Needs air, water, light and warmth to grow. Seed splits open, roots grow downwards. First shoot appears. Roots and shoots grow bigger. Leaves appear. Begin to make own food.

_____

_____

_____

_____

_____

_____

_____

_____

The word PHOTOSYNTHESIS comes from the Greek words 'phos' (which means light) and 'suntithenai' (which means to put together).

The following words all come from the Greek word 'phos'. Even though the spelling is different, the meaning of the root word still remains.

Write the meanings of these words. Use your dictionary to help you.

photocopier _____

photography _____

phototherapy _____

Getting Down to the Grass Roots

In the word sleuth below, find the twelve words which have these roots as their base. Write the words you find next to their correct root.

Aqua = water (Latin) _____

Portare = carry (Latin) _____

Corpus = body (Latin) _____

Caput = head (Latin) _____

Polis = city (Greek) _____

Pathos = feeling (Greek) _____

A	Y	H	T	A	P	M	Y	S	W	K
L	O	P	O	N	E	O	D	X	N	I
O	E	C	J	A	Z	Q	E	L	I	P
O	P	O	L	I	T	I	C	I	A	N
J	T	R	O	P	S	N	A	R	T	F
E	N	P	C	F	N	L	P	O	P	G
M	E	O	I	T	A	C	I	F	A	W
K	C	R	T	S	Y	W	T	I	C	B
S	I	A	E	C	I	T	A	U	Q	A
C	L	L	H	M	E	J	T	J	B	C
P	O	R	T	A	B	L	E	F	A	N
K	P	I	A	Q	U	A	L	U	N	G
S	E	V	P	G	C	O	R	P	S	E

Choose one word from each of the root word categories above.

Write it in a sentence which shows its meaning.

1. _____

2. _____

3. _____

4. _____

5. _____

6. _____

Befores and Afters

Match the following prefixes with the words in the box:

dis, il, de, ex, at, in, re, un, trans, im

possible, entangle, planted, tract, legal, side,
plain, compose, produce, usual

Fill in the missing spaces in the sentences below with the words you made.

1. Plants use brightly coloured petals to _____ insects.
2. These seedlings will need to be _____ soon.
3. Can you _____ the process of photosynthesis?
4. Please _____ the roots of this plant.
5. In some countries it is _____ to pick wildflowers.
6. Plant matter will _____ .
7. The Venus flytrap is an _____ plant because
   it eats insects.
8. It is _____ for plants to survive
   without water.
9. _____ every seed is a food supply.
10. Many plants _____ from seeds.

Choose the correct suffix for each word. Write the word you make in the correct box.

Take care - the spelling might change.

mouth, invent, perform, dirt, kind, noise, faith, ready, attend, celebrate,
confuse, sad, jealous, cup

ance	ness	ful
_____	_____	_____
_____	_____	_____

y		ion
dirty		_____
_____		_____
_____		_____

Super Spinach Saps Sailor's Strength!

Focus Points
- To punctuate correctly a formal letter.
- To identify idioms in a passage.
- To match idioms with their meanings.
- To use a dictionary to discover word origins.

Background Information
Letter of Complaint
A letter of complaint should be short and to the point. The address of the person writing the letter is written on the top right side of the page, the title and the address of the person receiving the letter is written on the left side of the page. If the person's name is not known, the greeting *Dear Sir/Madam* is used. Finish the letter with *Yours faithfully* or *Yours sincerely* and the writer's full name. No punctuation is used in the addresses. A comma is used after the greeting (Dear Sir,) and ending (Yours sincerely,).

Idioms
Idioms are sayings that do not mean what they seem to say. For example:
nip in the bud (means to stop something before it gets started); have a heart (means to take pity).

Subject Integration
Language: Write other formal letters: write away to a company asking for information for a school assignment, write a thankyou letter to a guest visitor to the school. Students keep lists of words that originate from other languages. Classify the words under different themes.

Occupations - chauffeur (F), chef (F), jackaroo (Aus)

Make a class book of idioms. Each student illustrates a literal translation of an idiom.

Answers
Super Spinach
Saps Sailor's
Strength!

17 Strong street
Superheroland

2nd September 1995

Public Affairs Assistant
Super Foods Company Ltd
PO Box 45
Foodtown

Dear Sir or Madam ,
    I am writing to complain about your product Super Spinach I have found it to be a real lemon. Your advertising promises super human energy immediately upon ingestion but I have found this to be untrue.
    I used your product last week when I was called upon to save a beautiful maiden from a chicken-hearted villain. To my embarrassment, your product left me in a real stew.
    I wash my hands of Super Spinach and request that you send a full refund to the address above.

    Yours faithfully,
    Sapped Sailor

1. a real lemon 2. chicken-hearted 3. a real stew 4. wash my hands

This is a Piece of Cake!: 1. D 2. E 3. A 4. C 5. B
1. someone you want to marry 2. by not stirring up any trouble 3. being suspicious of someone or something 4. a secret 5. somewhere crowded

A Smorgasboard of Food
Across: 5. muesli - Swiss 9. café - French 12. éclair - French 13. escargot - French 15. caviar - French 16. soufflé - French 17. schnitzel - German
Down: 1. mousse - French 2. gâteau - French 3. shishkebab - Turkish 4. quiche - French 6. strudel - German 7. gelato - Italian 8. macaroni - Italian 10. yoghurt - Turkish 11. entrée - French 14. sushi - Japan

Super Spinach Saps Sailor's Strength!

Punctuate the letter below by circling the letters that should be capital letters and putting in the commas and full stops.

17 strong street
superheroland

2nd september 1995

public affairs assistant
super foods company ltd
po box 45
foodtown

dear sir or madam

 I am writing to complain about your product Super Spinach I have found it to be a real lemon your advertising promises super human energy immediately upon ingestion but I have found this to be untrue

 I used your product last week when I was called upon to save a beautiful maiden from a chicken-hearted villain to my embarrassment, your product left me in a real stew

 I wash my hands of Super Spinach and request that you send a full refund to the address above

yours faithfully

sapped sailor

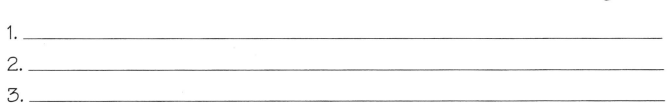

Can you find the idioms in the letter above? Write them below.

1. _____

2. _____

3. _____

4. _____

This is a Piece of Cake!

Read these idioms. Match them with their meanings below.

1. out of sorts • _____
2. keep a straight face • _____
3. pull someone's leg • _____
4. hit the nail on the head • _____
5. get into hot water • _____

(a) to trick someone/ play a joke on someone
(b) to get into trouble
(c) to arrive at the correct conclusion
(d) not well
(e) to try not to laugh

Answer these questions:

1. Who would you pop the question to?

    _____

2. How can you let sleeping dogs lie?

    _____

3. What would you be doing if you smelt a rat?

    _____

4. What would you be giving away if you let the cat out of the bag?

    _____

5. Where would you be if you were packed like sardines? _____

Draw a picture which shows the literal meaning of each of these idioms.

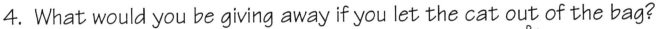

raining cats and dogs	catch your breath	pick your brains	having a bee in one's bonnet

A SMORGASBORD OF FOOD!

Many of the words we use that have to do with food have come from other languages. Work out what each word in the puzzle is and use your dictionary to help you discover the language it originated from. The first letter of the answer is written after the clue. One has been done for you.

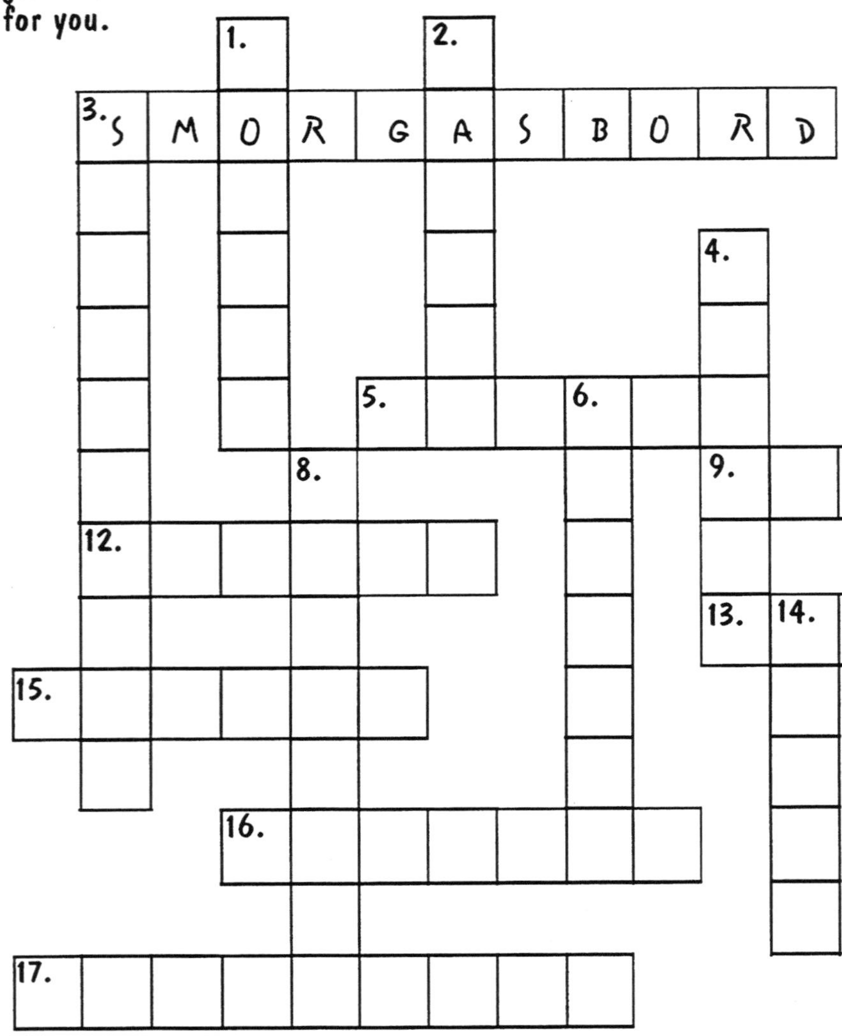

ACROSS

3. a buffet meal of different hot and cold dishes (S) Swedish
5. a cereal made of different products (M) ____________
9. a small restaurant which serves light meals (C) ____________
12. a sweet pastry filled with cream or custard (E) ____________
13. edible snail usually eaten with a sauce (E) ____________
15. the roe of certain fish which has been pressed and salted (C) ____________
16. a light, fluffy dish made with eggs (S) ____________
17. a thin slice of meat (S) ____________

DOWN

1. a chilled dessert made with whipped cream and eggs (M) ____________
2. a cake with a sponge or pastry base decorated with cream, fruit etc (G) ____________
3. grilled and marinated pieces of meat on a skewer (S) ____________
4. a savoury tart (Q) ____________
6. a rolled pastry with a filling (S) ____________
7. an iced confection (G) ____________
8. dried hollow tubes of pasta (M) ____________
10. a food made from milk that has been curdled (Y) ____________
11. a dish served before a main course (E) ____________
14. a dish consisting of small bundles of rice served with a topping like raw fish (S) ____________

Teachers Notes

The Story of a Baseball Player

Focus Points
- To order sentences in the correct sequence.
- To recall information from a passage.
- To identify the parts of speech in a sentence.
- To revise the use of nouns, verbs, adverbs and adjectives.
- To locate synonyms and antonyms.

Background Information
Biography
A biography is an account of a person's life written by someone else. It should consist of factual information and contain: an introduction about the person, including birth date; their life story in correct sequence; conclusion.

Nouns
Nouns are the names of people, animals, places, things or feelings.
There are four types of nouns.

> Common: names of people, animals, places or things (bone, dog, brother).
> Proper: names of particular people, animals, places or things (London, Tuesday, Mary). Proper nouns begin with a capital letter.
> Collective: names of groups of things (bunch, flock, team).
> Abstract: names of feelings or ideas (sadness, beauty, fear).

Verbs
Every sentence must have a verb. Verbs are doing, being or having words.
Simple verbs have only one word. *I ate the hamburger. Max kicked the football.*
Compound verbs consist of two or more words. *The snake is slithering away. He will play tomorrow.*
Auxiliary (helping) verbs make up the first part of compound verbs. Auxiliary verbs are usually different forms of the verbs **to be** or **to have** (am, is, are, had, has, have). Others used are shall, will, may or do.
Compound verbs are also known as verb phrases.
All verbs change according to tense. The tense refers to whether the action is happening now (present tense), will happen in the future (future tense), or has already happened (past tense). *She is jumping.* (present tense) *She will jump.* (future tense)
She jumped. (past tense).

Adjectives
Adjectives are words that describe nouns or pronouns.
They tell us:
what kind (*He ate a small apple*); how many (*She has two sisters*); what position (*He was the third caller*); what colour (*Daniel liked the red kite*); which one (*I want that book*).

Adverbs
Adverbs tell us more about verbs. They tell us how, when or where.
(*Samantha drove slowly.* (tells us how) *He will be leaving tomorrow.* (tells us when) *The baby crawled outside.* (tells us where)
Many adverbs are made by adding "ly" to adjectives (sweetly, happily, slowly).

Conjunctions
Conjunctions are words used to join words, phrases or sentences together. Some examples of frequently used conjunctions are: *and, because, but, where, after, unless.*

Prepositions
A preposition is a word that shows the relationship between nouns or pronouns and other words. They are often found in front of the nouns or pronouns: *on the table; through the park; with our family.*
There are many prepositions. Here are some examples of words that can be used as prepositions: *after, before, by, during, from, in, on, off, through, upon, within.*

Synonyms and Antonyms
A synonym is a word which has a similar meaning to another word: reply - respond, answer; stare - gape, glare.
An antonym is a word which is opposite in meaning to another word: possible - impossible; sell - buy.

Subject Integration
Language: Discuss the differences between an autobiography and a biography. Research and write the biography of another famous sportsperson. Students write their autobiography. Make word sleuths or word tags using synonyms and antonyms.

Answers
The Story of a Baseball Player
5,2,1,4,3 1902 - He was sent to a Baltimore orphanage. 1935 - Babe Ruth retired. 1923 - Yankee Stadium was opened. 1947 - He established the Babe Ruth Foundation. 1948 - He died of cancer OR He made his last appearance at the Yankee Stadium.
Which Part of Speech?
1. adjective 2. preposition 3. proper noun 4. verb 5. adverb 6. pronoun 7. adverb 8. common noun 9. verb 10. proper noun 11. pronoun 12. conjunction 13. verb 14. adjective 15. common noun 16. conjunction 17. proper noun 18. adjective 19. pronoun 20. preposition
1. beauty, beautify, beautifully 2. pacify, peaceful, peacefully 3. danger, endanger, dangerous 4. width, wide, widely 5. strength, strengthen, strongly
Opposites Attract
1. career 2. last 3. famous 4. attracted 5. help 6. established. Word Search: 1. overact 2. turmoil 3. lively 4. young 5. grief 6. fear 7. rear 8. rigid 9. dismiss 10. sour 11. ready 12. yes 13. struggle 14. expose 15. expire 16. extra 17. abandon 18. night 19. tight 20. true.

Learning Solutions

The Story of a Baseball Player

Read the biography below.

Babe Ruth was a famous <u>American</u> baseball player. He was the highest paid baseball player of his time. He was born George Herman Ruth, <u>in</u> <u>Baltimore</u>, USA, in 1895. At the age of seven <u>he</u> <u>was</u> sent to a Baltimore orphanage where he <u>first</u> learned to play baseball.

<u>He</u> began to play <u>professionally</u> in 1914 and later that <u>year</u> was sold to the Boston Red Sox as a pitcher. In 1920 he <u>joined</u> the New York Yankees. When <u>Yankee Stadium</u> opened in 1923 <u>it</u> was nicknamed 'the House that Ruth Built' <u>because</u> of the great number of fans he <u>attracted</u>. In 1927 he set a record of 60 <u>home</u> runs.

During his baseball <u>career</u> he set or equalled 76 pitching <u>and</u> batting records. He retired in 1935. He established the <u>Babe Ruth</u> <u>Foundation</u> to help <u>underprivileged</u> children in 1947. <u>His</u> last appearance, before he died <u>of</u> cancer in 1948, was at the Yankee Stadium on its 25th anniversary, eight weeks before his death.

The following sentences are about the life of Babe Ruth. Number them in the correct order.

☐	He died of cancer.
☐	He was signed up by the Boston Red Sox as a pitcher.
☐	He was sent to a Baltimore orphanage.
☐	He appeared at the Yankee Stadium on its 25th anniversary.
☐	He set a record of 60 home runs.

Why are these dates important?

1902 _____

1935 _____

1923 _____

1947 _____

1948 _____

Learning Solutions

Which Part of Speech?

Which part of speech is each underlined word in the biography?

It is either a noun, verb, adjective, adverb, pronoun, conjunction or preposition.

If it is a noun, write what type of noun it is.

1. American _____
2. in _____
3. Baltimore _____
4. was sent _____
5. first _____
6. He _____
7. professionally _____
8. year _____
9. joined _____
10. Yankee Stadium _____
11. it _____
12. because _____
13. attracted _____
14. home _____
15. career _____
16. and _____
17. Babe Ruth Foundation _____
18. underprivileged _____
19. His _____
20. of _____

Complete this table.

	NOUN	VERB	ADJECTIVE	ADVERB
1.			beautiful	
2.	peace			
3.				dangerously
4.		widen		
5.			strong	

OPPOSITES ATTRACT

Find words in the biography which mean almost the same as these.

1. profession _____   2. final _____
3. renowned _____   4. drew _____
5. assist _____   6. created _____

Rewrite these sentences replacing the underlined words with a suitable synonymn.

1. Babe Ruth was a <u>great</u> baseball player.
   _____

2. He <u>stopped</u> playing baseball in 1935.
   _____

3. When he was <u>little</u> he was <u>sent</u> to an orphanage.
   _____

4. He was <u>idolised</u> <u>especially</u> by children.
   _____

5. He established the Babe Ruth Foundation
   for <u>underprivileged</u> children.
   _____
   _____

6. He was one of the first five players <u>elected</u>
   for the Baseball Hall of Fame.
   _____

Find the antonyms of these words in the Tag Wordsearch. The last letter of the word you have just found is the first letter of the next word. The first one has been done for you.

1. underplay
2. peace
3. inactive
4. mature
5. happiness
6. courage
7. front
8. flexible
9. retain
10. sweet
11. unprepared
12. no
13. ease
14. conceal
15. begin
16. essential
17. support
18. day
19. loose
20. false

O	B	I	G	E	T	L	I	V	E	L	Y	A	M	A	P
V	E	U	R	T	I	E	X	L	X	L	O	N	E	I	R
E	N	O	E	O	H	G	G	U	P	S	U	D	C	E	A
R	D	P	M	A	P	G	Y	M	O	I	N	K	A	V	E
A	I	R	U	S	U	S	I	T	S	O	G	R	I	E	F
C	U	C	M	R	T	R	O	T	E	X	P	I	R	E	L
T	A	G	T	B	E	U	G	H	A	C	E	G	O	X	O
E	N	S	L	A	N	O	N	G	P	A	L	I	S	T	W
N	D	E	D	E	W	S	S	I	M	S	I	D	I	R	G
T	L	Y	S	E	N	T	A	N	O	D	N	A	B	A	Y

Teachers Notes

Annual General Meeting

Focus Points
- To read and complete the minutes of an Annual General Meeting.
- To indicate the mood for given sentences and write own sentences to demonstrate understanding.
- To explain the meaning of given proverbs and write others correctly.

Background Information
Mood
The mood indicates how a verb is expressed in a sentence.
An interrogative mood refers to the action of a verb as a question. *Do you want a drink?*
An indicative mood refers to the action of a verb as giving facts. *He found it at the beach.*
An imperative mood refers to the action of a verb as an instruction or command. *Take it now!*
A subjunctive mood refers to the action of a verb as doubtful, wishful or possible. *He may come with us.*

Proverb
A proverb is a popular saying used to express some truth or wisdom.

Subject Integration
Class Organisation: Meetings
Hold monthly class meetings to establish and enforce class rules or to form a fund-raising body or social group. Elect office bearers, etc. Investigate terms such as quorum, delegate, unanimous, rescind and motion. Establish protocol associated with meetings, such as the role of the chairperson and voting procedures. Have students attend an official school meeting to see procedures in action.

Writing
Proverb Match
Write several proverbs on strips of paper and cut in half. | A stitch in time | saves nine.

Students draw strips and find the matching half of their proverbs, or select a strip and write a short story which ends with that proverb.

Comic Display
Encourage students to bring comics to display. Develop language activities using the comics, such as comprehension cards, word sleuths and characterisations.

Answers
HOW WAS IT SAID?
interrogative, indicative, interrogative, subjunctive, imperative, indicative, subjunctive, subjunctive
MIXED UP RIDDLES
A bird in the hand is worth two in the bush – Tom. You can lead a horse to water but you can't make it drink – Casper. Let sleeping dogs lie – Yogi. The grass is always greener on the other side of the fence – Scrooge McDuck. One man's meat is another man's poison – Popeye. Don't put all your eggs in one basket – Bugs Bunny. A rolling stone gathers no moss – Batman. People in glass houses shouldn't throw stones – Fred Flintstone.

ANNUAL GENERAL MEETING
FOR COMIC BOOK CHARACTERS

Date: 12/3/96

Meeting Opened: 7.45 p.m.

Present: Batman, Wonder Woman, Tom, Aladdin, Casper, Archie, Donald Duck, Jerry, Robin, Yogi Bear, Minnie, Superman, Scrooge McDuck, Bugs Bunny, Little Mermaid, Mickey Mouse, Fred Flintstone, Charlie Brown, Beauty.

Apologies: Spiderman, Winnie the Pooh, Road Runner, Daffy Duck.

Correspondence: In

1) Letter from Spiderman expressing regret about the poor quality of the super heroes masks he supplied for the Annual Ball.
2) Postcard from Daffy Duck – on holiday in Hawaii.

Out

1) Memo to Winnie asking him to provide more honey for next beach picnic to be held in June.
2) _____
   _____

Election of Office Bearers:

Chairperson Minnie thanked all outgoing office bearers and vacated the chair. Yogi Bear took the chair and called for nominations for Chairperson, Secretary and Treasurer.

Chairperson:

Charlie Brown nominated Wonder Woman, she declined.

Little Mermaid nominated Bugs Bunny, seconded by Mickey Mouse.

With no further nominations, Bugs Bunny was elected.

Secretary:

_____
_____
_____

Treasurer:

Archie nominated Casper, seconded by Beauty.

With no further nominations, Casper the Friendly Ghost was elected.

General Business:

1) Scrooge passed a motion 'that all comics be reduced in price by 20% by the end of the year', seconded by Donald. On a show of hands the motion was rescinded.
2) Casper expressed concern for the level of violence in comic books. Mickey and Archie agreed. Mickey offered to support Casper in a bid to confront the publishers and reduce the number of violent acts committed by characters in a given story.
3) _____
   _____
   _____
4) _____
   _____
   _____
5) _____
   _____

• With no further general business the meeting closed at 10.25 p.m.

How Was it Said?

Use the information in the minutes to complete these speech bubbles.

Show these moods.

Imperative   **Interrogative**   **Indicative**   **Subjunctive**

Underline the verbs in these sentences and indicate the mood.

CASPER: I <u>believe</u> the level of violence in some comics <u>is</u> too high.   *Indicative*

SUPERMAN: Are you referring to my comic?

CASPER: Yes, and there are many others which I think are too violent.

BEAUTY: Have you any suggestions? Can we improve this problem?

YOGI: I think we should look very carefully at this problem, but I hope we can eat first.

CASPER: Yogi Bear! Control yourself!

YOGI: But I'm starving.

BEAUTY: Supper might be served later, Yogi. If I were you I'd just concentrate on the meeting. Otherwise Casper might get violent.

SUPERMAN: That'd be very interesting, Beauty. But I don't think it will happen.

Write a sentence for each character which indicates these moods.

CASPER:	_____	INDICATIVE
BEAUTY:	_____	INDICATIVE
YOGI:	_____	IMPERATIVE
SUPERMAN:	_____	INTERROGATIVE
CASPER:	_____	IMPERATIVE
BEAUTY:	_____	SUBJUNCTIVE
SUPERMAN:	_____	SUBJUNCTIVE

43

Learning Solutions

Mixed Up Riddles

Match each riddled proverb with a character.
Write the correct proverb on the line.

Yogi •   • You can coax a ghost to a haunted house but you can't make it scare you.

_____

Fred Flintstone •   • A mouse in the hand is worth two in the trap.

_____

Bugs Bunny •   • Let sleeping bears lie.

_____

Tom •   • The money is always greener on the other side of the bank vault.

_____

Casper •   • One man's spinach is another man's meat.

_____

Scrooge McDuck •   • Don't put all your carrots in one basket.

_____

Popeye •   • A rolling riddler gathers no jokes.

_____

Batman •   • People in stone houses shouldn't throw grass.

_____

Explain the meaning of these proverbs.

A fool and his money
are soon parted!

_____

When in Rome, do as
the Romans do.

_____

As you make your bed,
so you must lie in it.

_____

A barking dog never
bites.

_____

Ship Ahoy!

Focus Points
- To understand the purpose of a diary.
- To complete entries in a diary.
- To complete exercises in noun and verb agreement.
- To play the game 'Treasure on Trigger Island' and correctly identify the subject and predicate in each sentence.

Background Information
Diaries/Journals
Diaries and journals contain a personal record of daily/weekly events.

Subject and Verb Agreement
A verb must agree with its subject in number as well as person. If the subject is singular then the verb must be singular. *The boy was crying.*

A plural subject has a plural verb. *The boys were crying.*

When there are two singular nouns joined by 'and', a plural verb is required. *Matthew and Lisa are going to the library.*

Expressions such as *each, anyone, anybody, anything, every, everyone, nobody, one of, none of,* and *neither of* are followed by a singular verb.

Use a singular verb with collective nouns when it refers to the group as a whole. *The crew is sick* but *Most of the crew are sick.*

Two singular verbs joined by *neither... nor* and *either... or* take a singular verb. *Neither James nor Jack was at school.*

Subject and Predicate
Sentences have two parts - a subject and a predicate. The subject tells us the person or object we have written about. To identify the subject in a sentence, first identify the verb. Then ask *who* or *what*. The answer is the subject. The rest of the sentence, including the verb, is the predicate.

Subject Integration
Language
Write diaries for fictional characters such as Little Red Riding Hood or Superman. Pretend to be a pirate, explorer or space traveller and send a postcard or letter to a loved one.

Maths
Design a treasure map. Ask a friend to use the scale and clues you have given to see if they can find the hidden treasure.

Answers
Ship Ahoy!
May 1st 1762: has, are, is
May 5th 1762: were, were, feels
May 9th 1762: is, have, am

Ship Ahoy!

Read this diary kept by a pirate. Circle the correct words in each sentence. Write two more entries in the diary.

May 1st 1762

What a piece of good luck! Captain One-Eye (has, have) found Greenbeard's Treasure map! We (is, are) setting sail for Trigger Island to discover the treasure! The crew (is, are) very excited!

May 5th 1762

The Revenge went through a rough storm last night. The waves (was, were) as tall as the ship's mast. Young Jake and William Galley, the chief gunner, (was, were) killed. We lost the water barrels overboard. Everyone (feel, feels) quite ill today.

May 9th 1762

Drinking water (is, are) low. Fights (have, has) broken out over the water rations. Neither Captain One-Eye nor I (am, are) ready to give up yet! We should sight land soon!

_____

_____

_____

_____

_____

_____

_____

_____

Learning Solutions

Search For the Hidden Treasure !

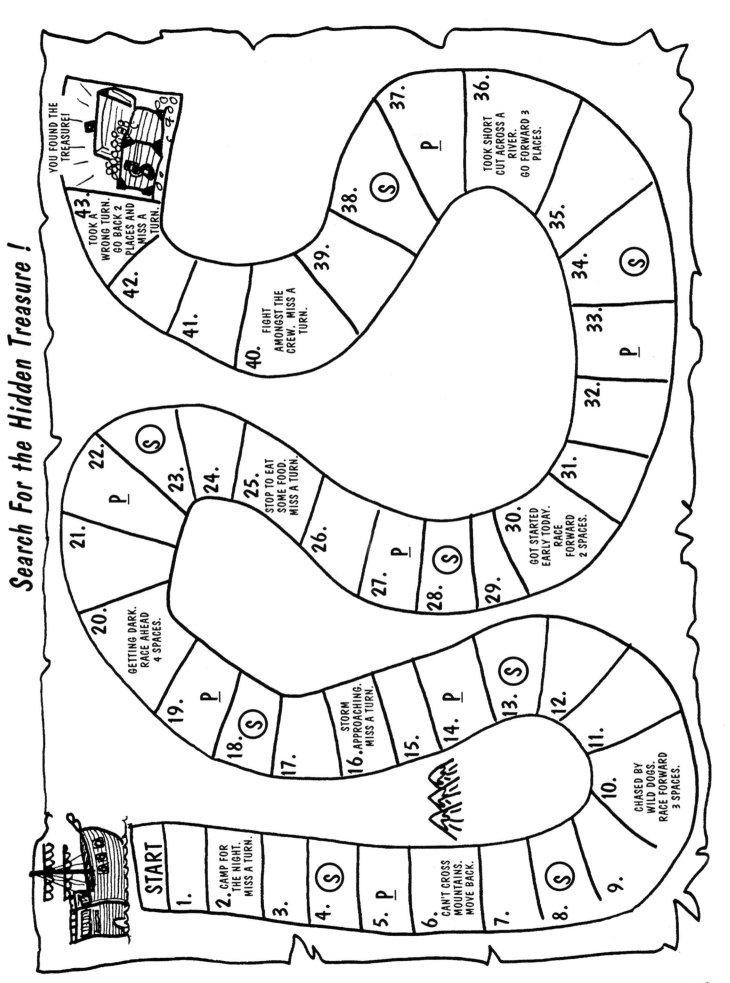

YOU FOUND THE TREASURE!

43. TOOK A WRONG TURN. GO BACK 2 PLACES AND MISS A TURN.

42.
41.
40. FIGHT AMONGST THE CREW. MISS A TURN.
39.
38.
37.
36. TOOK SHORT CUT ACROSS A RIVER. GO FORWARD 3 PLACES.
35.
34.
33.
32.
31.
30. GOT STARTED EARLY TODAY. RACE FORWARD 2 SPACES.
29.
28.
27.
26.
25. STOP TO EAT SOME FOOD. MISS A TURN.
24.
23.
22.
21.
20. GETTING DARK. RACE AHEAD 4 SPACES.
19.
18.
17.
16. STORM APPROACHING. MISS A TURN.
15.
14.
13.
12.
11.
10. CHASED BY WILD DOGS. RACE FORWARD 3 SPACES.
9.
8.
7.
6. CAN'T CROSS MOUNTAINS. MOVE BACK.
5.
4.
3.
2. CAMP FOR THE NIGHT. MISS A TURN.
1.
START

Treasure
on Trigger Island

The game 'Treasure on Trigger Island' is a game for 2-4 players. You will need a dice and each player needs a coloured marker. You need to photocopy the sheet onto thick card and cut out the sentences below to use in the game.

Players take turns to throw the dice and move that number of spaces. Follow the instructions on the game. If you land on an S or P, the player on your left must pick up a card and read you the sentence. You must correctly identify either the subject of the sentence (if you landed on S) or the predicate (if you landed on P). If you cannot identify the subject or predicate, you must move back to where you were. The winner of the game is the first person to reach FINISH.

(The treasure chest) is full of gold and precious jewels.	(It) is buried near Skull Rocks.
On the high seas, (pirate ships) of all sizes can be found.	Hundreds of years ago (pirates) roamed the seas.
(Great nations) have been founded by sea rovers.	(Blackbeard) was the terror of the seas.
(Captain Kidd) was one of the most famous pirates of all times.	There were (some jewels) in the treasure chest.
Slowly (they) made their way to the island.	(We) are setting sail for Skull Island.
(Pirates) would frighten many people.	Into the Deadly Sea, sailed (the pirate ship Revenge.)
There is (a high mountain) behind Dead Man's Point.	(Captain Kidd and his crew) are sailing in their ship.
(The seas) were too rough.	(The pirate) carried several pistols.
In the treasure chest there was (a map.)	(Most of the pirates) felt very sick.
(The waves) were as tall as the ship's mast.	(They) lost the water barrels overboard.

Learning Solutions

Get Away to Coral Island!

Focus Points
- To add details to a travel advertisement.
- To punctuate sentences using colons and semicolons.
- To complete a postcard.
- To identify and finish similes.
- To insert quotation marks in sentences.
- To recognise the difference between direct and indirect speech.

Background Information
Semicolons
Semicolons are used instead of full stops to show the link between two balanced ideas in a sentence.

I enjoyed my holiday; I met so many people.

They are also used to separate long items in a list.

We saw a towering plateau at Nulu National Park; unique plant life at the Gasper Gorges; and a clear, running creek at Yeda Crossing.

Colons
Colons are used to introduce lists, quotations and phrases.

On your holiday you need to remember to bring: your swimming costume, a towel, sunscreen, a hat and insect repellent.

Similes
Similes are expressions which are used to compare people or things. Often the words 'like' or 'as' are used.

As strong as an ox, as sweet as honey.

Quotation Marks
Quotation marks are used to show exactly what has been said by a speaker.

"I saw the accident," said the pedestrian.

They are not used in indirect speech.

The pedestrian said that he saw the accident.

Subject Integration
Art/Craft
Students design a travel brochure for a place they have visited. Study commercial travel brochures to get ideas.

Social Studies
Students choose a country to research and present important facts for a travel book. Include population, climate, geography, places to visit.

Language
Students pretend that they are visiting the country they have researched and write a postcard to send to their family or friends at home. Students role-play conversations. They then write them down and punctuate them correctly.

Answers
Get Away to Coral Island
1. Don't go too close to the edge of the cliff; you could fall over. 2. Coral Island is breathtakingly beautiful; it's a great place to visit. 3. First we went swimming; then we went snorkelling 4. I was tired; so I went home. 5. The fish are very tame; they are used to being handfed by visitors.

P.S. I Miss You!
as clear as crystal, as brown as a berry
1. pancake 2. daisy 3. thieves 4. cucumber 5. nails 6. gold
1. mouse 2. fox 3. snail 4. bird 5. eel 6. ape

Indirectly Speaking
2. Sue asked her if she was going to London soon.
3. He commented that the weather was beautiful there.
4. I asked the guide how far it was to the next town.
5. Anna said that we could go snorkelling or water skiing on Long Island.
1. "When are you leaving on your holiday?" asked Joe.
2. Lucy grumbled, "I hope we haven't missed our flight. You're very late."
3. "If you continue on that road," explained the tour guide, "you will reach the town of Franklin."
4. "What a beautiful sunset!" exclaimed Lucy. "Let's go for a walk along the beach."
1. Lucy asked, "What shall we do today?"
"I'd like to take a cruise to Grand Island," replied Kate. "What would you like to do?"
"That sounds great," said Lucy. "Let's go there today."
2. "Where did you go on your holiday?" Anna asked her friend, Matt.
"John and I went to Coral Island," Matt replied. "It was fantastic."
"What did you do there?" asked Anna.
"We went snorkelling and swimming," said Matt.

GET AWAY TO CORAL ISLAND!

For your next holiday choose one of the remaining natural wonders of the world!

On Coral Island you can see magnificent waterfalls; _____

_____

_____

Choose your accommodation. We have these available: chalets, caravans, _____

_____

_____

You'll have a wonderful time; _____

_____

Choose from a wide range of activities: swimming, snorkelling, _____

_____

_____

*8 days /7 nights from £499

Contact your travel agent now!

*Subject to conditions.

Finish these sentences. The first one has been done for you.

1. I have travelled to: _Phuket, Bali, Coral Island and Honolulu._

   _____

2. These are the activities available on Coral Island: _____

   _____

3. On our trip we saw: _____

   _____

4. When going on a holiday you need to bring: _____

   _____

5. I bought these souvenirs: _____

   _____

Punctuate these sentences using semicolons.

1. Don't go too close to the edge of the cliff you could fall over.
2. Coral Island is breathtakingly beautiful it's a great place to visit.
3. First we went swimming then we went snorkelling.
4. I was tired so I went home.
5. The fish are very tame they are used to being handfed by visitors.

P.S. I miss you!

Pretend that you are visiting Coral Island. Finish this postcard to send to your family back home. Address the postcard correctly.

Dear Mum and Dad,

    We arrived on Saturday. The island is magnificent. The water is as clear as crystal. We've been swimming every day and I'm already as brown as a berry. We're having such a great time! _____

_____

_____

_____

_____

              Love from

             _____

P.S. I miss you! _____

Affix stamp here

Find the similes written in the postcard. Underline them.

Complete these similes by choosing a word from the box below.

1. As flat as a _____ .
2. As fresh as a _____ .
3. As thick as _____ .
4. As cool as a _____ .
5. As hard as _____ .
6. As good as _____ .

thieves, cucumber, gold, pancake, nails, daisy

Try to work out these similes. The answers are all animals.

1. As timid as a _____ .
2. As cunning as a _____ .
3. As slow as a _____ .
4. As free as a _____ .
5. As slippery as an _____ .
6. As hairy as an _____ .

Indirectly Speaking

Change these into indirect speech. The first one has been done for you.

1. John said, "I want to go on a holiday."
   <u>John said that he wanted to go on a holiday.</u>

2. "Will you be going to London soon?" Sue asked her.
   _____

3. "The weather is beautiful there," he commented.
   _____

4. I asked the guide, "How far is it to the next town?"
   _____

5. Anna said, "We could go snorkelling or water skiing on Long Island."
   _____

Put quotation marks and other necessary punctuation in these sentences.

1. when are you leaving on your holiday asked joe
   _____

2. lucy grumbled I hope we haven't missed our flight you're very late
   _____

3. if you continue on that road explained the tour guide you will reach the town of franklin
   _____

4. what a beautiful sunset exclaimed lucy let's go for a walk along the beach
   _____

Write out these conversations again. Put in quotation marks and other necessary punctuation. Give each new speaker a new line.

1. lucy asked what shall we do today I'd like to take a cruise to grand island replied kate what would you like to do that sounds great said lucy let's go there today
   _____
   _____
   _____
   _____

2. where did you go on your holiday anna asked her friend matt john and I went to coral island matt replied it was fantastic what did you do there asked anna we went snorkelling and swimming said matt
   _____
   _____
   _____

Read the Label

Focus Points
- To rewrite the information from product labels to include only the main ideas.
- To complete a table and indicate which verbs are transitive or intransitive.
- To differentiate between active and passive voice.
- To identify compound and simple verbs.

Background Information
Transitive Verbs
Transitive verbs have a direct object. That is, a noun, pronoun or a clause, the whom or what of the action. In the sentence, *I like puppies*, **like** is a transitive verb because puppies is the object. WHAT or WHOM is liked? Answer – puppies.

Intransitive Verbs
Intransitive verbs have no direct object. That is, there is no noun or pronoun to direct the action of the verb. In, *The cat ate the bird*, **the bird** is the object. But in, *The cat ate slowly*, there is no object to direct the verb, therefore **ate** is intransitive.

Active and Passive Voice
If the subject of a sentence is the doer of the action, then the voice is active. In, *The cat ate the bird*, **the cat** is the subject and is the doer, so the voice is active. But in, *The bird was eaten by the cat*, **the bird** is the subject but it is being acted upon by **the cat**, therefore the voice is passive.

Simple and Compound Verbs
Simple verbs are one word. I **eat** breakfast. You **were** good. He **ran** fast.
Compound verbs consist of an auxiliary verb and a present or past participle. The auxiliary verbs are helpers from the verbs **to be** and **to have**. She **has eaten** her breakfast. You **are going** to be good.

Answers
Spaghetti Sauce
sliced: object - onion (noun) - transitive. tossed: object - it (pronoun) - transitive.
cooked: no object - intransitive. poured: object - can of tomatoes (noun) - transitive.
stirred: no object - intransitive. added: object - herbs (noun) - transitive.
left: object - the pot (noun) - transitive. simmer: no object - intransitive.

VERB	DIRECT OBJECT	TRANSITIVE OR INTRANSITIVE
are	none	intransitive
allow	air	transitive
to ventilate	none	intransitive
keep	it	transitive
open	none	intransitive
applying	none	intransitive
clean	skin	transitive
dry	none	intransitive
tear	none	intransitive
pull	thread	transitive
remove	tabs	transitive
place	none	intransitive
press	none	intransitive
to adhere	the plaster	transitive
keep	wound	transitive
change	none	intransitive
bathing	none	intransitive
to promote	healing	transitive

Verb Express
2) compound 3) compound 4) simple 5) simple 6) compound 7) simple 8) compound 9) simple 10) compound
to write, to know, to choose, to go, to fly, to lie
2) A 3) P 4) A 5) A 6) A 7) P 8) A 9) A 10) P
grieve-mourn, astonish-amaze, join-connect, allow-permit, guess-estimate, elevate-raise, break-fracture, forgive-pardon, inhibit-prohibit, partake-participate
1) hose 2) scrub 3) dry 4) wax, 5) polish
1) scrape 2) wash 3) rinse 4) drain 5) dry
1) cut 2) pin 3) sew 4) hem 5) wear
1) boil 2) pour 3) brew 4) squeeze 5) drink

Read the Label

THIS GARMENT IS ABLE TO BE WASHED IN A WASHING
MACHINE ON THE WARM AND GENTLE CYCLE. HOWEVER,
DO NOT USE BLEACH ON THIS MATERIAL AS THE COLOUR MAY RUN OR FADE.
THIS GARMENT MAY BE TUMBLE DRIED BUT ONLY ON THE WARM SETTING.
IT IS POSSIBLE BUT NOT ADVISABLE TO IRON THIS MATERIAL. FOR BEST
RESULTS PLEASE ENSURE THE IRON IS WARM.
THIS GARMENT MAY BE TAKEN TO A DRY-CLEANER AS THE MATERIAL CAN
WITHSTAND THE DRY-CLEANING PROCESS. HOWEVER, SPOT DRY-CLEAN FIRST
TO ENSURE THE GARMENT WILL NOT BE SPOILED.

WARM MACHINE WASH
DO NOT BLEACH
TUMBLE DRY WARM
WARM IRON
DRY-CLEANABLE

BOLD ON MOULD

THIS PRODUCT ABSOLUTELY DESTROYS MOULD
AND MILDEW AND INGRAINED DIRT. IT IS LETHAL
ON ALL SURFACES AND HELPS TO REMOVE
BUILT UP SOAP SCUM.

THIS PRODUCT CAN OCCASIONALLY CAUSE
STAINING AND DISCOLOUR CERTAIN SURFACES.
DO NOT USE ON METAL SURFACES, UNGLAZED
TILES, UNPAINTED WALLS, LAMINATED
SURFACES, COLOURED FABRICS, DAMAGED
PAINT SURFACES OR ANY DETERIORATED
ENAMEL SURFACES. IT IS ADVISABLE TO SPOT
TEST BEFORE APPLYING TO ANY HOUSEHOLD
SURFACE.

USE IN THE LAUNDRY TROUGH, ON ALL FLOORS,
TOILET SEATS, TOILET BOWLS, TOILET FLOORS,
ALL BATHROOM SURFACES, SHOWER HEAD,
SHOWER RECESS, BATH,
BATHROOM FLOOR, AROUND TAPS, ON PLASTIC
SHOWER CURTAINS. SUITABLE FOR ALL MOULD
AFFECTED AREAS SUCH AS THE RUNNERS ON
DOORS, SHOWER SCREENS, ALL WET AREAS
AND THE KITCHEN SINK.

SPRAY OIL

INGREDIENTS: MIXED
VEGETABLE OILS.
NO CHOLESTEROL, SALT.
NO ADDED COLOURS OR
FLAVOURS.
IDEAL FOR ALL COOKING
SURFACES.
DON'T SPRAY NEAR NAKED
FLAME OR INHALE THE
CONTENTS OF THIS CAN.

Elaborate on the important
information in this label.

SPRAY OIL

_____
_____
_____
_____
_____
_____
_____
_____
_____

Rewrite this label using only the important information.

BOLD ON MOULD

_____
_____
_____
_____
_____
_____
_____
_____
_____

Spaghetti Sauce

Mum sliced an onion and tossed it around in the melted butter until cooked. When cooked, she poured a can of tomatoes into the pot. She stirred slowly. She added herbs then left the pot to simmer slowly.

VERB	DIRECT OBJECT	TRANSITIVE	INTRANSITIVE
sliced	an onion (noun)	✔	
tossed	it (pronoun)	✔	
cooked	?		✔
poured	a can (noun)	✔	
stirred	?		✔
added			
left			
simmer			

Bandaids are suitable for minor cuts and sores. They allow air to ventilate around the wound and keep it free of dirt and water.
Do not open before applying.
Before use:
Clean skin and dry thoroughly.
Instructions:
Tear along top, pull thread down and remove tabs. Place over area.
Press down gently to adhere the bandaid to the skin.
Keep wound clean and change daily after bathing to promote faster healing.

VERB	DIRECT OBJECT	TRANSITIVE OR INTRANSITIVE
are	none	intransitive
allow	air	transitive

Verb Express

Underline the verbs in these sentences. Write simple or compound after each.

1) Trent <u>ate</u> an apple. _____simple_____
2) Sam was playing basketball. _____
3) Mum is driving the car. _____
4) Aunt Betty has a pet goat. _____
5) I am twelve years old. _____
6) Sue has had her injection. _____
7) I like peppermint sticks. _____
8) They were waiting for the rain to stop. _____
9) She loves her guinea pig. _____
10) Tomorrow we will be going hiking. _____

Write the infinitive for these verbs.

arose   – to arise
written   _____
knew   _____
chose   _____
gone   _____
flying   _____
lain   _____

Write A = active voice, or P = passive voice in the box for these sentences.

P	1)	The horse was ridden by Brendon.
	2)	Tom kicked the football.
	3)	The dog was tied up by its owner.
	4)	The cat climbed the tree.
	5)	The telephone rang loudly.
	6)	Mary picked the flowers.
	7)	That fence was painted yesterday.
	8)	Dad sat under the pergola.
	9)	Dianne was reading her book.
	10)	Francis was hit by a car.

Match these verbs with similar meanings.

to instruct   to raise
to grieve   to prohibit
to astonish   to participate
to join   to permit
to allow   to mourn
to guess   to teach
to elevate   to fracture
to break   to pardon
to forgive   to connect
to inhibit   to amaze
to partake   to estimate

Find meanings for these verbs.

to foreclose _____
to foreshadow _____
to forecast _____
to forejudge _____
to forego _____
to forearm _____

Number these verbs in order.

MAKE A CAKE

bake [3]   mix [1]   pour [2]   cool [4]   eat [5]

WASH A CAR

scrub [ ]   dry [ ]   hose [ ]   polish [ ]   wax [ ]

WASH THE DISHES

rinse [ ]   wash [ ]   drain [ ]   dry [ ]   scrape [ ]

MAKE A DRESS

sew [ ]   hem [ ]   cut [ ]   pin [ ]   wear [ ]

MAKE A CUP OF TEA

boil [ ]   drink [ ]   pour [ ]   squeeze [ ]   brew [ ]

Learning Solutions

Teachers Notes

By Phone or Fax

Focus Points
- To examine the use of language in everyday messages and greetings.
- To rewrite a telephone message, a note and a greeting card using more appropriate language.
- To distinguish between longhand and shorthand language.

Background Information
Shorthand Language
The presence of computers and other sophisticated machines has altered the speed at which letters and messages can be received. A facsimile message or electronic mailing direct to a computer terminal has alleviated the stack of mail a person used to receive. In keeping with this trend, the use of shorthand language has become necessary in order to maximise output. A faster pace in general has reduced the need for long-winded, grammatically correct letters and messages.

As well as the shorthand language, many signs, symbols, acronyms and abbreviations are now apparent. For example, an employer may direct an employee to 'FLAG ME ASAP!' which roughly translates as, I would like you to inform me or notify me as soon as possible. It is important that students acknowledge and understand the need to use shorthand language in certain situations.

Subject Integration
Poetry
Time line
Collect and read examples of poetry from different periods — for example the Romantic Era, 18th and 19th centuries. Examine the use of language and the evolution of the English language. Make a time line of poetry pieces.

Writing
Antique or Modern
Many language reference books contain lists of antique language. Brainstorm lists and have students write letters, messages or notes using the antique forms.

Examples of antique language and the modern equivalent are: *thenceforth - from that time on; betwixt - between; clomb - climbed; howbeit - nevertheless; ken - knowledge; moon - a month; fare - to travel; whilom - once upon a time.*

Glossary
Handbooks for machines, and glossaries contain jargon and terms pertinent to topics. Have students write a glossary of terms for a science experiment, a computer program, a recipe or a rugby game.

Environmental print
Look in newspapers, magazines, handbooks and at the graffiti on walls. Collect examples of shorthand language and write or paste them into a scrapbook.

Answers
By Phone or Fax
NO number, FAX facsimile, ASAP as soon as possible, PK pack, XMAS Christmas, MAC Macintosh, COL colour, RE with reference to, RMS reams, COMP. computer, CO. company.

Greetings
Kate, I can't wait to see the new home! I will meet you at my business office 5 p.m. Wednesday. I hope you take my advice. I have already received a great offer for your house. Your Friendly Estate Agent, Marie.

There's a Better Way To Say It
viz - namely; @ - at; ... - ellipsis - and so on; i.e. - that is (id est); © - copyright; pro rata - in relation to a rate; e.g. (exempli gratia) - for example; £ - pound; ® - registered; ™ - trademark, % - a percentage; LTD - a limited company

checkout girl - sales assistant, old man - an elderly gentleman, crippled - physically challenged, a looney - a mentally disturbed person, ugly - unattractive, a mistake - an error, poor - underprivileged, skinny - underweight, false teeth - dentures, dead - deceased, car crash - road accident.

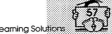

By Phone or Fax

9-NOV-97 MON 9.42   COMPUTER WHOLESALERS   FAX NO: (1244) 554432   P.01

TO: TONY DEAN   FROM: Marty Jones, Computer Wholesalers
ADDRESS: 90 Newholm St   ADDRESS: 9 Kilmore Road
                CHESTER, CH2 3QS   CHESTER, CH2 3QS
                                               TEL NO: (1244) 345520
NO OF PAGES: 1   DATE: 9 NOV 1997

RE: DELAY WITH SUPPLY OF EQUIP FOR APPLE MAC

TONY,
TRACE ORDER – NO DELIVERY AS YET.
ORDER NO. 67B9055
•   PK 10 HD DISKS
•   XMAS CLIP ART
•   3 RMS LAS. PAPER – NO 576   COL. RED
                         – NO 573   COL. YEL

FOLLOW UP PLEASE – WANT ASAP!
MARTY
SALES CO. EXEC
COMP. WHOLESALERS

FAX MESSAGE

Read this message. Underline all the shorthand language used. Write the longhand versions for these.

NO _____   ASAP _____

FAX _____   XMAS _____

PK _____   COL _____

MAC _____   COMP _____

RE _____   CO _____

RMS _____

Write the longhand for this telephone message.

> **While you were out, someone telephoned:**
> **Who?** Craig Coxon
>
> **Message:**
> Can't make training tomorrow pm
> He'll ring back, but if can't catch you,
> you ring him pm today or am tomorrow
> **Urgent** - needs to discuss strategies
> before tomorrow pm.

_____

_____

_____

_____

Learning Solutions

Greetings

Kate,
Can't weight I see the knew home!
Will meat you at me business office
5 am wensday arvo. Hope your
take my advise I have all ready
recieved a grate offer four you
house.

Your frendly
Really Estate Agent
Marie

Can you help Ari, Marie's assistant, who has just arrived from Australia, to correct his spelling and grammar before this note is sent to Kate Travers.

_____
_____
_____
_____
_____
_____
_____

When you read Pete's birthday message it is obvious that he is a very good friend of Sam's. Complete the birthday message from Sam's mother.

Sammy,

The old grey stallion ain't
what he used to be
It must be scary to be
pushin' 50
Chin up old fella
Don't croak it when ya
blow the candles out!
Have a great day mate!

Pete

Dear Sam

Happy Birthday

Write a longhand version for this message.

LETTERGRAM

Congrats – you've tied the knot!
Wish we were there. Good luck!
Aunt Chris and Uncle Mike

LETTERGRAM

There's a Better Way to Say it !

Use a dictionary to find out the meaning of these shorthand terms and signs.

viz _____   @ _____   ... _____

i.e. _____   © _____   pro rata _____

e.g. _____   £ _____   ® _____

TM _____   % _____   LTD _____

Match these words with a better alternative.

checkout girl   deceased
old man   dentures
crippled   road accident
a looney   underweight
ugly   underprivileged
a mistake   elderly gentleman
poor   unattractive
skinny   an error
false teeth   a sales assistant
dead   physically challenged
car crash   a mentally disturbed person

Write alternatives for these.

fat
_____

short
_____

daggy
_____

whacko
_____

pimples
_____

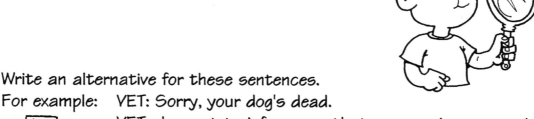

Write an alternative for these sentences.
For example: VET: Sorry, your dog's dead.
                VET: I regret to inform you that your canine companion has
                     passed away.

TEACHER: Get out of my class!
TEACHER: _____

BROTHER: This game will blow your mind.
BROTHER: _____

SISTER: You're a liar!
SISTER: _____

MAN: That's the ugliest baby I've ever seen.
MAN: _____

GIRL: She is so dumb.
GIRL: _____

DOCTOR: This disease is going to kill you.
DOCTOR: _____

60 Learning Solutions